The plays of Maurice Maeterlinck • Maurice Maeterlinck

Publisher's Note

The book descriptions we ask book-sellers to display prominently warn that this is an historic book with numerous typos, missing text, images and indexes.

We scanned this book using character recognition software that includes an automated spell check. Our software is 99 percent accurate if the book is in good condition. However, we do understand that even one percent can be a very annoying number of typos! And sometimes all or part of a page is missing from our copy of a book. Or the paper may be so discolored from age that you can no longer read the type. Please accept our sincere apologies.

After we re-typeset and design a book, the page numbers change so the old index and table of contents no longer work. Therefore, we often remove them.

We would like to manually proof read and fix the typos and indexes, manually scan and add any illustrations, and track down another copy of the book to add any missing text. But our books sell so few copies, you would have to pay up to a thousand dollars for the book as a result.

Therefore, whenever possible, we let our customers download a free copy of the original typo-free scanned book. Simply enter the barcode number from the back cover of the paperback in the Free Book form at www.general-books. net. You may also qualify for a free trial membership in our book club to download up to four books for free. Simply enter the barcode number from the back cover onto the membership form on the same page. The book club entitles you to select from more than a million books at no additional charge. Simply enter the title or subject onto the search form to find the books.

If you have any questions, could you please be so kind as to consult our Frequently Asked Questions page at www. general-books.net/faqs.cfm? You are al-

so welcome to contact us t. General Books LLC™, Me 2012. ISBN: 97811501896

❧ ❧ ❧ ❧ ❧ ❧ ·

Modern Symbolism and Ma...... Maeterlinck.

IN a broad sense, all language is symbolism and all art is language. To the artist the material universe is a medium through which to express the immaterial realities of thought and feeling. There cannot be art except where the two elements are present together, — the immaterial passion, action or reflection, and the material embodiment by which it is made manifest through the senses to the instinct, intelligence and imagination of humanity. The one is the symbol — it would not exceed the modesty of prose to say, the sacrament of the other.

But Symbolism, as the name of a school, evidently demands a narrower definition. It must be distinguished from Realism on the one hand, and from Expressionism on the other, and these distinctions arise from radical psychological differences in men. Without presuming to divide mankind by hard and fast lines into classes, it may be said generally that there are three ways of looking at the world, and that every indi vidual adopts one of these ways predominantly. There are those of " yellow primrose " celebrity, who see the material appearance and nothing beside. To another class the impression of the sensible object is relatively faint, and the important thing seems to be the idea, the general principle. The third type concerns itself chiefly with people, and has a tendency in many cases to conceive even inanimate things as having a fictitious kind of personality. The first is the natural, the second the ethical, the third the poetic mind. One views the world as thing, one as law, or abstract intelligence, one as personality. Not that any one has one of these outlooks to the ab-

r two. The as all that. ’ard anothilosophies ilike veer, ...u ait veers with them. If the thing be uppermost in men's minds, we shall have an imitative and realistic output; if the soul, a poetic, perhaps even a dramatic one. If the abstract idea dominate, art turns to symbolism of necessity. The body is its own majestic speech, and the emotions of the soul have their instinctive and spontaneous language, but for the idea expression must be forcibly created. The life and the heart find utterance through natural correspondences, — metaphors that exist by the constitution of things; but for the mental we must find artificial correspondences, allegories, and consciously invented symbols.

As with everything else, there is a rhythm in the recurrence of artistic schools. This idea seems to be true, though popular. But the recurrence is never in exactly the same form. The symbolism of to-day, diverse as are the forms it takes in the work of Mallarm6 in France, of Maeterlinck in Belgium, of Gilbert Parker in England, and Bliss Carman in America, has yet a general character that differentiates it from the symbolism of other periods. It by no means of necessity involves a complete and consistent allegory. Its events, its personages, its sentences rather imply than definitely state an esoteric meaning. The story, whether romantic as "The Seven Princesses" or realistic as "The Intruder," lives for itself and produces no impression of being a masquerade of moralities; but behind every incident, almost behind every phrase, one is aware of a lurking universality, the adumbration of greater things. One is given an impression of the thing symbolized rather than a formulation. Not only is the allegory not reached by the primitive device of personification, but it shows no trace of being in any way made to order. It is an allegory that will never bite anybody—but the Browning societies. Instead of looking at marionettes with most gross and palpable strings, we see a living picture, with actuality and motive sufficient to itself, while yet we cannot rid ourselves of the haunting presence of vast figures in the wings. It is perfectly clear that the invisible "Intruder" is Death, that "The Blind" is the symbol of a world lost in the dark forest of unfaith and unknowledge, — its ancient guide, the Church, sitting dead in the midst of the devotees and them of little faith, who all alike have lost the swift vision of the intuition and can inform themselves of their situation only by the slow uncertain groping of the reason. In vain they seek for a guide in animal instinct, in the glimmer of vision possessed by the poet,— who turns aside and gathers flowers, — in some power of insight fancied in insanity, in the newborn future that cannot utter yet its revelation. But these correspondences must not be pursued too curiously. They are intended to appeal to the imagination and the emotions, not to the mere ingenuity of the intellect.

In this new movement Maeterlinck is not alone. Such symbolism, suggestive rather than cut-and-dried, is the same that Gilbert Parker uses in "Pierre and His People." So in one of the stories in that volume the Man and the Stone, existing primarily for their own simple terrific story, are lifted up at the same time into Titanic primitive types. Charles G. D. Roberts' tales of animals, such as "The Young Ravens that call upon Him," are symbolic in the same way, not with the artificial symbolism of " Esop's Fables" and "Reineke Fuchs," but by revealing in the simple truth of animal life a universal meaning. The symbol is not invented; the thing is found to be symbolic. This, if not the final word of poetry, has always been its first word, and it promises well for the poetic quality of the literature that is to be, that the strongest of the young writers of to-day have a tendency to mythmaking.

This is the more convincing, that this movement is not the imitation by the many of the eccentricities of one, but the spontaneous and independent development, in writers alien in race, residence, and experience, of similar traits and methods. It is possible, of course, though not probable, that Ibsen was under the influence of Maeterlinck to some extent in writing "The Master-Builder,"—a play of sheer symbolism if ever one was written. Mallarme, probably the greatest French poet since Hugo; is surrounded by an enthusiastic circle of disciples, and Maeterlinck may have fallen under the charm of his personality and his conversation. And yet, barring the symbolic principle which they hold in common, it would be difficult to find two writers more unlike than Maeterlinck and Mallarm£. William Sharp's "Vistas" and Oscar Wilde's "Salom6" might perhaps not have been written had the authors been less familiar with the contemporary literature of the Continent. But Carman, Roberts, and Parker have evidently reached their results without any communication with France or Belgium. Their work is saner, fresher, and less morbid. The clear air of the lakes and prairies of Canada blows through it. It has not the kind of likeness that comes of imitation, and I doubt if one of the three has ever given any special consideration to Maeterlinck, or is familiar with his books.

Symbolism, then, is not a school, in the sense of a clique. It is a drift in art, that has of late years begun to set in wherever the arts flourish. It is obtaining in painting, among the most extreme radicals, as well as in literature. It would be interesting to trace the connection between English Pre-Raphaelitism and the new movement, between the pictures of the *ecole symboliste* and those of Watts and Burne-Jones, between the new poets and Rossetti; but it is my intention here rather to indicate some of the points that are suggested by the new school, than to pursue any of them exhaustively.

Two things individualize Maeterlinck from the rest of the school, — the peculiarity of his technique, and the limitation of his emotional range. His conceptions are romantic to the last degree, and so also is their setting, except perhaps in "L'Intruse" and "Interieur;" but the dialogue is written in a language of the simplest realism. His vocabulary usually, except in some of the stage directions, though chosen with nicety, is hardly more copious than that of a peasant. The simple iteration character- istic of all real conversation, but especially of the conversation of Frenchmen, is imitated to an extent to which even Dumas pere, who was a master of its effectiveness, never pushed it. But this iteration is not used merely for the sake of realism. It is part of a general appreciation and effective use of the principle of parallelism in art.

Parallelism has been better understood in decorative art than in any other. Its value for expression has been but meagrely recognized. In poetry, since its magnificent uses by the Hebrews, it has been chiefly confined to its most artificial form of antithesis and to the subordinating and decorative purposes of metre and rhyme. Maeterlinck is almost, if not quite alone among modern writers in so using it as to confirm the general dictum of Delsarte for all the arts, that parallelism, in its usual uses a principle of convention, of weakness, or of subordination, may become, simply by being carried a step further, a powerful instrument to express the shadowland of human emotions.

For his use of iterations of phrase in the dialogue, Maeterlinck has been criticised more severely than for anything else he has done. It has been called "mere Ollendorf" and held up to unsparing ridicule. But in almost every instance the reviewers who have waxed so facetious, have supported their position by quoting snatches of dialogue isolated from all connection with the scene of which they are part and which is their justification. In no case have they indicated the exceptional circumstances, the emotions of amazement, of horror, of hysterical fear, which accompany the extreme instances they cite. Not that I would claim any literary impeccability for Maeterlinck; far from it. He walks continually on the dangerous border between the tragic and the ridiculous, and it would be strange indeed if he never made a misstep; but in the main it must be confessed that he has a cool head and a sure footing. He has been accused of a lack of humor, but it is rather a restriction to one kind of humor, — the hysterical mirth of tragic crises, the grin on the everlasting skull.

For this is the other characteristic that separates Maeterlinck from his fellows, — his restriction, whether voluntary or of necessity, to a single mood. His master-tone is always terror' — terror, too, of one type, — that of the churchyard. If other emotions are presented, they are transposed into this key. He is a poet of the sepulchre, like Poe, — as masterly in his own method as Poe was in his, and destined, perhaps, to exert the same wide influence. His devotion to the wormy side of things may prevent him from ever becoming popular; yet Poe's ghastly tales won more than a narrow circle of readers, and "Dr. Jekyll and Mr. Hyde" crowded the theatres. At any rate, whether M. Maeterlinck's subjects please or not, the method which he and the others whom I have mentioned have adopted, is not likely to become obsolete as long as the world still hearkens to the parables of the Man of Nazareth.

Richard Hovey.

Princess Maleine.

Persons.

HjALMAR, *King of one part of Holland,*

Marcellus, *King of another fart of Holland.*

Prince Hjalmar, *son of* King Hjalmar.

Little Allan, *son of* Queen Anne.

Angus, *friend of* Prince Hjalmar.

Stephano,) _ *officers of* MARCELLUS.
Vanox, J

A Chamberlain.

A Physician.

A Madman.

Three Poor Men.

Two Old Peasants, A Cowherd.

Lords, Officers, A Cook, A Cripple, Pilgrims,

Peasants, Servants, Beggars, Vagabonds,

Children, Etc. Anne, *Queen of Jut-* land. Godeliva, *wife of* King Marcellus.

Princess Maleine, *daughter of* Marcellus *and*

Godeliva.

Princess Uglyane, *daughter of* Queen Anne.

Maleine's Nurse.

Seven Nuns.

An Old Woman.

Maids Of Honor, Servants, Peasant-Women, Etc.

A big black dog called Pluto.

The first Act is at Harlingen; the others at the castle of Ysselmonde and its neighborhood.

Princess Maleine.

ACT FIRST.

Scene I. — *The gardens of the castle.*

Enter Stephano *and* Vanox.

Vanox.

What time is it?

STEPHANO.

It must be midnight, judging by the moon.

VANOX.

I think it will rain.

STEPHANO.

Yes; there are great clouds in the west. We shall not be relieved until the fete is ended.

VANOX.

That will not be before daybreak.

STEPHANO.

Oh! oh! Vanox!

Here a comet appears over the castle.

VANOX.

What?

STEPHANO.

Again the comet of the other night!

VANOX.

It is enormous.

STEPHANO.

It looks as though it dripped blood on the castle.

Here a shower of stars seems to fall upon the castle. VANOX.

The stars are falling on the castle! Look! look! look!

STEPHANO.

I never saw such a shower of stars! You would say Heaven wept over this betrothal.

VANOX.

They say all this presages great disasters.

STEPHANO.

Yes, — wars, perhaps, or the death of kings. Such omens were observed when the old king Marcellus died.

VANOX.

They say those stars with long girl's-hair announce the death of princesses.

STEPHANO.

They say... they say many things.

VANOX.

Princess Maleine will dread the future.

STEPHANO.

In her place, I should dread the future without the warning of the stars.

VANOX.

Yes; old Hjalmar seems to me strange enough....

STEPHANO.

Old Hjalmar? Listen: I dare not say all I know; but one of my uncles is chamberlain to Hjalmar. Well, then, if I had a daughter, I would not give her to Prince Hjalmar.

VANOX.

I don't know.... Prince Hjalmar....

STEPHANO.

Oh! It is not on account of Prince Hjalmar, but his father!...

VANOX.

They say that his wits...

STEPHANO.

Ever since that strange Queen Anne came from Jutland, where she was dethroned, after the old king, her husband, had been cast into prison, — ever since she came to Ysselmonde, they have been saying... they have been saying... in short, old Hjalmar is more than seventy years old, and I think he loves her rather too much for his age.

VANOX.

Oh! Oh!

STEPHANO.

That is what they say. — And I dare not speak all I know. — But do not forget what I have said to-day.

VANOX.

Then, poor little princess!

STEPHANO.

Oh, I do not like the look of this betrothal! See, it is raining already!

VANOX.

And perhaps a storm, yonder. A bad night. *An* Attendant *passes with a lantern.* How goes the fete?

Attendant. Look at the windows.

VANOX.

Oh, the lights are not out there.

ATTENDANT.

And will not be to-night. I never saw such a revel. Old King Hjalmar is absolutely drunk. He kissed pur King Marcellus, he.,, VANOX.

And the betrothed couple?

ATTENDANT.

Oh! the betrothed couple are not drinking much. Well, good-night. I am going to the kitchen. They are not drinking plain water down there, either.... Goodnight.

Exit Attendant.

Vanox.

The sky is turning black, and the moon is strangely red.

STEPHANO.

It rains torrents. Now, while the rest drink, let us...

Here the brilliantly lighted windows of the castle, at the further end of the garden, suddenly fly to pieces. Cries, rumors, tumult.

VANOX.

Ohl STEPHANO.

What is the matter?

VANOX.

They are smashing the windows!

STEPHANO.

Afire!

VANOX.

They are fighting in the hall.

Princess Maleine, dishevelled and in tears, is seen running past at the further end of the garden.

STEPHANO,

The Princess!

VANOX.

Where is she running?

STEPHANO.

She is weeping.

VANOX.

They are fighting in the hall.

STEPHANO.

Let us go see.

Cries, uproar; the gardens fill with officers, servants, etc. The doors of the castle are violently flung open, and King Hjalmar appears on the steps, surrounded by courtiers and halberdiers. Above the castle, the comet. The shower of stars continues.

KING HJALMAR.

Ignoble Marcellus! You have done a monstrous thing to-day. Gome, my horses, my horses! I am going! I am going! I am going! And I leave you your Maleine, with her green face and her white eyelashes! And I leave you with your old Godeliva. But wait! You shall go on your knees across your marshes. And I shall come to celebrate your betrothal with all my halberdiers and all the ravens in Holland for the funereal feast. Let us be gone! We shall meet again. Ha! Ha! Ha!...

Exit, with his Courtiers.

Scene II. — *An apartment in the castle.*

Queen Godeliva, Princess Maleine, *and* Nurse *discovered at their spinning-wheels, singing.*

The nuns are lying sick,

Lying sick — it is their hour —

The nuns are lying sick,

Lying sick in the tower.

GODELIVA.

Come, weep no more, Maleine; dry your tears and go down into the garden. It is noon.

Nurse.

That's just what I've been telling her all the morning, madam! What's the use of spoiling your eyes? When she opened her window this morning, she looked out at a road that leads to the forest and fell a-crying. Then I asked her, "Are you looking already at the road that leads to the tower, Maleine?" GODELIVA.

Po not speak of that, NURSE.

Oh, yes, though; we must speak of it; there will be much speaking of it by and by. Well, then, I asked: "Are you looking already at the road that leads to the tower where they once shut up the poor Duchess Anne because she loved a prince they would not let her love?" GODELIVA.

Do not speak of that.

NURSE.

On the contrary, we must speak of it; there will be much speaking of it by and by. Well, then, I asked... Here comes the King.

Enter Marcellus. MARCELLUS.

Well, Maleine?

MALEINE.

Sire?

MARCELLUS.

Did you love Prince Hjalmar?

MALEINE.

I did, sire. MARCELLUS'.

Poor child! But do you love him still?

MALEINE.

I do, sire.

MARCELLUS.

You love him still?

MALEINE.

I do.

MARCELLUS.

You love him still, after...

GODELIVA.

My lord, do not frighten her!

MARCELLUS.

I am not frightening her!... See here, I come as a true father should, and I am thinking only of your happiness, Maleine. Let us look at this dispassionately. You know what has happened: old King Hjalmar has outraged me without reason; or, rather, I guess his reasons only too well. He has shamefully affronted your mother, he has insulted you more basely still, and had he not been my guest, had he not been there under the hand of God, he would never have gone forth from my castle! Well, never mind that now. — But is it with us you should be angry? With your mother? With me? Come now, answer, Maleine?

MALEINE.

No, sire.

MARCELLUS.

Then what is the use of weeping? As for Prince Hjalmar, it is better you should forget him henceforth. Besides, how could you love him seriously! You have hardly seen each other. And at your age the heart is like wax; it can be fashioned as you will. Hjalmar's name was as yet written only in the clouds, a storm has risen and washed it all away; from this night you will think of it no more. Besides, do you believe you would have been really happy at Hjalmar's court? I do not mean the Prince; the Prince is but a child; but his father. You know well enough that people are afraid to speak of him; you know well enough that there is not a more gloomy court in Holland; you know that his castle has perhaps strange secrets. But you do not know what folk say of that alien Queen who has come with her daughter to the castle of Ysselmonde, and I will not repeat what they say; for I would not pour poison into your heart. — But you were about to enter, all alone, a fearful forest of intrigue and suspicion. — Come now, answer, Maleine.. Did not all this alarm you? And was it not a little against your will that you were going to espouse Prince Hjalmar?

MALEINE.

No, sire, MARCEIXUS.

Very well. But now answer me frankly. Old King Hjalmar must not be allowed to triumph. We are going to have a great war on your account, Maleine. I know that Hjalmar's ships surround Ysselmonde and are about to sail, perhaps before the full moon; on the other hand, the Duke of Burgundy, who has loved you for a long time... *turning to the* Queen... I do not know whether your mother...

GODELIVA.

Yes, my lord.

MARCEIXUS.

Well?

GODELIVA.

She should be prepared little by little....

MARCEIXUS.

Let her speak!... Well, Maleine?

MALEINE.

Sire?

MARCELLUS.

You do not understand?

MALEINE.

What, sire?

MARCEIXUS.

You promise me to forget Hjalmar?

MALEINE.

Sire...

MARCELLUS.

You say? — You still love Hjalmar?

MALEINE.

I do, sire.

MARCELLUS.

"I do, sire!" Oh! devils and tempests! She avows that impudently; she dares to tell me that without shame. She has seen Hjalmar once only, for one single afternoon, and now she is hotter than hell.

GODELIVA.

My lord!

MARCELLUS.

Be silent. "I do, sire!" And she is not yet fifteen! Oh, one could kill them on the spot! For fifteen years I have only lived for her! For fifteen years I have held my breath in her presence! For fifteen years we have hardly dared to breathe for fear of her troubled glance! For fifteen years I have turned my court into a convent; and the day when I come to look into her heart...

GODELIVA.

My lord I...

NURSE.

May she not love, like another? Are you going to put her under glass? Is this any reason to scream at the top of your voice at a child? She has done nothing wrong!

MARCELLUS.

Oh! she has done nothing wrong!... Now, in the first place, you hold your peace,... I am not speaking to you, and it is doubtless at your prompting, you go-between...

GODELIVA.

My lord!

NURSE.

Go-between! — I, a go-between!

MARCELLUS.

Will you ever let me speak? Begone! begone, both of you! Oh! I know well enough you have put your heads together, and that the era of intrigues has begun now, — but wait! —. Begone, begone! Oh! tears, tears! *Exeunt* Godeliva *and* Nurse. Now, then, Maleine, first close the doors. Now that we are alone, I wish to forget all. They have been giving you bad advice, and I know that among themselves women form strange projects. Not that I have anything against Prince Hjalmar; but you must be reasonable. Do you promise me to be reasonable?

MALEINE.

Yes, sire.

MARCELLUS.

Ah! you see! Then you will not think any longer of this marriage?...

MALEINE.

Yes.

MARCELLUS.

Yes? — You mean you will forget Hjalmar?

MALEINE.

No.

MARCELLUS.

You do not yet renounce Hjalmar?

MALEINE.

No.

MARCELLUS.

And if I compel you? And if I imprison you? And if I separate you forever from your Hjalmar with his little girl's face? What say you? *She weeps.* Ah! So! Begone; we shall see! Begone!

Exeunt separately. Scene III. — *A forest. Enter* Prince Hjalmar *and* Angus.

PRINCE HJALMAR.

I was sick; and the stench of all those dead bodies! the stench of all those dead bodies! And now I feel as though the night and the forest had sprinkled a little water on my eyes....

ANGUS.

Nothing remains but the trees.

HJALMAR.

Did you see old King Marcellus die?

ANGUS.

No, but I saw something else. Yesterday evening, in your absence, they set fire to the castle, and old Queen Godeliva ran through the flames with the servants. They threw themselves into the ditches, and I think they all perished.

HJALMAR.

And Princess Maleine? Was she there?

ANGUS.

I did not see her.

HJALMAR.

Did the others?

ANGUS.

Nobody saw her; no one knows where she is.

HJALMAR.

She is dead?

ANGUS.

They say she is dead.

HJALMAR.

My father is terrible!

ANGUS.

Did you love her already?

HJALMAR.

Whom?

ANGUS.

Princess Maleine?

HJALMAR.

I saw her only once... But yet she had a way of casting down her eyes — and of folding her hands — so — and strange white eyelashes! — And her look! It was as though one were suddenly in a great pool of fresh water... I do not remember very well; but I should like to see that strange look once again.

ANGUS.

What is that tower on the knoll yonder?

HJALMAR.

It looks like an old windmill; it has no windows.

ANGUS.

There is an inscription on this side.

HJALMAR.

An inscription?

ANGUS.

Yes... in Latin.

HJALMAR.

Can you read it?

ANGUS.

Yes; but it is very old. Let me see: —
Olim inclusa
Anna ducissa
Anno...
there is too much moss over all the rest.

HJALMAR.

Let us sit down here.

ANGUS.

"*Ducissa Anna* " — that is the name of the mother of your betrothed.

HJALMAR.

Of Uglyane's mother? — Yes.

ANGUS.

That was a "yes" slower and colder than snow.

HJALMAR.

Good Lord! the time for a "yes" of flame is far enough from me now.

ANGUS.

Yet Uglyane is pretty.

HJALMAR.

I am afraid of her.

ANGUS.

Oh!

HJALMAR.

There is a little kitchen-maid's soul at the bottom of her green eyes.

ANGUS.

Oh! oh! But then, why do you consent?

HJALMAR.

What good not to consent? I am sick to die of it one of these twenty-thousand nights we have to live; and I want rest! rest! rest! Besides... whether it be she or another who will call me "darling Hjalmar," in the moonlight, while she pinches my nose... what matters? Faugh! —

Have you noticed my father's sudden fits of anger, since Queen Anne came to Ysselmonde? I do not know what is going on; but there is something wrong; and I am beginning to have strange suspicions. I am afraid of the Queen.

ANGUS.

And yet she loves you like a son.

HJALMAR.

Like a son?... I cannot say; and I have strange thoughts. She is more beautiful than her daughter, and that is a great evil at the outset. She is working like a mole at I know not what; she has roused my poor old father against Marcellus, and she has let loose this war. There is something underneath it all.

ANGUS.

There is. She wants to make you marry Uglyane. There is nothing infernal in that.

HJALMAR.

There is something else.

ANGUS.

Oh! I know! Once married she will send you to Jutland to fight on the icebergs for the little throne she usurped; and to deliver her poor husband, perhaps, who must be very uneasy, waiting for her. For when so beautiful a queen is wandering alone about the world, of course there must be episodes.

HJALMAR.

There is something else.

ANGUS.

What?

HJALMAR.

You will know some day. Let us go.

ANGUS.

Toward the city?

HJALMAR.

Toward the city? There is no longer a city; there is no longer anything but corpses between the crumbled walls!
_Exeunt.

Scene IV. — *A vaulted chamber in a tower.* Princess Maleine *and* Nurse *discovered.* Nurse.

It is three days since I began working to loosen the stones of this tower, and I have not a nail left at the end of my poor fingers. You will be able to boast that you were the death of me. But there it is; you must disobey; you must escape from the palace, you must join Hjalmar.

And here we are, in this tower; here we are, between heaven and earth, above the trees of the forest! Did n't I warn you? Did n't I tell you so? I knew your father well enough. — Is it after the war that we are to be released?

MALEINE.

My father said so.

NURSE.

But this war will never end. How many days have we been in this tower? How many days have I seen neither moon nor sun? And wherever I lay my hands, I find mushrooms and bats; and I saw this morning we had no water left.

MALEINE.

This morning?

NURSE.

Ay, this morning. What are you laughing at? It is no laughing matter. If we do not succeed in getting this stone out to-day, there is nothing left for us but to say our prayers. My God! My God! What can I have done to be put into this tomb, with the rats and the spiders and the mushrooms? / did not rebel, I was not insolent, as you were! Would it have been so difficult to feign submission, and give up this weeping willow of a Hjalmar who would not lift his little finger to deliver us?

MALEINE.

Nurse!

NURSE.

Ay; nurse! I shall soon be nurse to the earthworms on your account. And to think that but for you I should be sitting quietly at this very moment in the kitchen, or warming myself in the sun in the garden, waiting for the bell to call me to breakfast! Good God! Good God! What can I have done that I... Oh! Maleine! Maleine! Maleine!

MALEINE.

What?

NURSE.

The stone!

MALEINE.

The...

NURSE.

Yes — it has moved.

MALEINE.

The stone has moved?

NURSE.

It has moved! It is loosened! The sunlight comes through the mortar! Look, look! There is some on my gown! There is some on my hands! There is some on your face! There is some on the walls! Put the lamp out. There is some everywhere. I am going to push the stone out.

MALEINE.

Does it still stick?

NURSE.

Yes, but it is nothing! there, in that corner; give me your spindle! Oh, it will not fall!...

MALEINE.

Can you see anything through the chinks?

NURSE.

Yes, yes! — no! only the sunlight.

MALEINE.

Is it sunlight?

NURSE.

Yes, yes, it is sunlight! Look, look! It is silver and pearls on my gown; and it is warm as milk on my hands!

MALEINE.

Let me look too!

NURSE.

Do you see anything?

MALEINE.

I am dazzled!

NURSE.

How strange that we see no trees! Let me look!

MALEINE.

Where is my mirror?

NURSE.

I see better.

MALEINE.

Do you see any trees?

NURSE.

No. We are probably above the trees. But there is wind a blowing. I am going to try to push the stone out. Oh! *They start back before the rays of sunlight that rush in, and remain silent a moment at the farther end of the room.* I cannot see any more.

MALEINE.

Go and look! Go and look! I am afraid.

NURSE.

Close your eyes. I think I am struck blind.

MALEINE.

I shall go and look myself.

NURSE.

Well?

MALEINE.

Oh! it is a furnace! and I have nothing but, red wheels in my eyes.

NURSE.

But don't you see anything?

MALEINE.

Not yet! Yes, yes! The sky is all blue. And the forest! Oh! the whole forest!...

NURSE.

Let me look!

MALEINE.

Wait! I am beginning to see.

NURSE.

Do you see the city?

MALEINE.

No.

NURSE.

And the castle?

MALEINE,

No.

NURSE.

It must be on the other side, MALEINE.
    And yet... There is the sea.

NURSE.

There is the sea?

MALEINE.

Yes, yes; the sea. It is green.

NURSE.

But, then, you ought to see the city, me look!

MALEINE.

I see the lighthouse!

NURSE.

You see the lighthouse?

MALEINE.

Yes; I think it is the lighthouse....

NURSE.

But, then, you ought to see the city.

MALEINE.

I do not see the city.

NURSE.

You do not see the city?

MALEINE.

I do not see the city.

NURSE.

You do not see the belfry?

MALEINE.

No.

NURSE.

This is extraordinary.

MALEINE. 1 see a ship, out at sea.

NURSE.

Is there a ship out at sea?

MALEINE.

With white sails!...

NURSE.

Where is it?

MALEINE.

Oh! the sea-wind is blowing through my hair! — But there are no more houses along the roads!

NURSE.

What? Do not speak outside so; I cannot hear a word.

MALEINE.

There are no more houses along the roads!

NURSE.

There are no more houses along the roads?

MALEINE.

There are no more steeples across the country!

NURSE.

There are no more steeples across the country?

MALEINE.

There are no more windmills on the meadows!

NURSE.

No more windmills on the meadows?

MALEINE.

I do not recognize anything.

NURSE.

Let me look.—There is not a single peasant left in the fields. Oh! the great stone bridge is down. — But what have they done to the drawbridges? There is a farm yonder that has been burned. — And another!— And another!—And another! And... Oh! Maleine! Maleine! Maleine!

MALEINE.

What?

NURSE.

Everything is burned! Everything is burned! Everything is burned!

MALEINE.

Everything is...?

NURSE.

Everything is burned, Maleine! Everything is burned! Oh! I see now!... There is nothing left.

MALEINE.

It is not true. Let me see 1 NURSE.

As far as the eye can reach, everything is burned. The whote city is nothing but a heap of black bricks! I can see nothing of the castle but the moats filled with stones. There is no man nor beast in the fields. Nothing but ravens in the meadows. Nothing but the trees left standing!

MALEINE.

Why, then...!

NURSE.

Oh!

ACT SECOND. Scene I. — *A forest.*

Enter Princess Maleine *and* Nurse.

MALEINE.

Oh! how dark it is here!

Nurse.

How dark? how dark? Is a forest lit up like a ball-room? I have seen forests darker than this, — and where there were wolves and wild boars. Indeed, I do not know that there are none here; but at least, thank Heaven, a little moonlight and starlight falls between the trees.

MALEINE.

Do you know the road now, nurse?

Nurse.

The road? No, indeed; I do not know the road. I never knew the road; do you suppose I know all the roads? You wanted to go to Ysselmonde; / followed you; and now see where you have brought us, after walking me for the last twelve hours up and down this iorest, where we shall die of hunger, unless we are devoured first by the bears and wild boars; and all that to go to Ysselmonde, where you will be finely received by Prince Hjalmar, when he sees you coming, skin and bones, as pale as a wax figure, and as poor as a beggar.

MALEINE.

Men!

Enter three Poor Men.

Poor MEN.

Good-evening.

NURSE.

Good-evening. Where are we?

FIRST POOR MAN.

In the forest.

SECOND POOR MAN.

What are you doing here?

NURSE.

We are lost.

SECOND POOR MAN.

Are you alone?

NURSE.

Yes — no, we are here with two men.

SECOND POOR MAN.

Where are they?

NURSE.

Looking for the road.

SECOND POOR MAN.

Are they far off?

NURSE.

No; they are coming back.

SECOND POOR MAN.

Who is that girl? Is she your daughter?

NURSE.

Yes, she is my daughter.

SECOND POOR MAN.

She does not say anything; is she dumb?

NURSE.

No; she is not of this country.

SECOND POOR MAN.

Your daughter is not of this country?

NURSE.

Yes, yes; she is, but she is ill.

SECOND POOR MAN.

She is thin. How old is she?

NURSE.

She is fifteen.

SECOND POOR MAN.

Ho! Ho! Then she is beginning to. Where are those two men?

NURSE.

They must be close by.

SECOND POOR MAN.

I hear nothing.

NURSE.

Because they are not making any noise.

SECOND POOR MAN.

Will you come with us?

THIRD POOR MAN.

Do not speak evil words in the forest.

MALEINE. *1*

Ask them the way to Ysselmonde.

NURSE.

Which is the way to Ysselmonde?

FIRST POOR MAN.

To Ysselmonde?

NURSE.

Yes.

FIRST POOR MAN.

That way.

MALEINE.

Ask them what has happened.

NURSE.

What has happened?

FIRST POOR MAN.

Happened?

NURSE.

Yes; there has been a war?

FIRST POOR MAN.

Yes; there has been a war.

MALEINE.

Ask them if it be true that the King and Queen are dead.

NURSE.

Is it true that the King and Queen are dead?

FIRST POOR MAN.

The King and Queen?

NURSE.

Yes; King Marcellus and Queen Godeliva.

FIRST POOR MAN.

Yes, I believe they are dead.

MALEINE.

They are dead?

SECOND POOR MAN.

Yes, I believe they are dead; everybody dead in that part of the country.

MALEINE.

But you do not know when they died?

SECOND POOR MAN.

No.

MALEINE.

You do not know how?

SECOND POOR MAN.

No.

THIRD POOR MAN.

The poor never know anything.

MALEINE.

Have you seen Prince Hjalmar?

FIRST POOR MAN.

Yes.

SECOND POOR MAN.

He is going to be married.

MALEINE.

Prince Hjalmar going to be married?

SECOND POOR MAN.

Yes.

MALEINE.

To whom?

FIRST POOR MAN.

I don't know.

MALEINE.

When is he going to be married?

SECOND POOR MAN.

I don't know.

NURSE.

Where could we sleep to night?

SECOND POOR MAN.

With us.

FIRST POUR MAN.

Go to the hermit's.

NURSE.

What hermit?

FIRST POOR MAN.

Below there at the cross-roads of the "four Judases." NURSE.

At the cross-roads of the "four Judases"?

THIRD POOR MAN.

Don't shriek that name so in the darkness.

Exeunt, Scene II. — *A hall in the castle. King Hjalmar and Queen Anne discovered, embracing.* ANNE.

My glorious conqueror!

KING.

Anne! *Kisses her.* ANNE.

Hush! Your son!

Enter Prince Hjalmar; *he goes to an open window, without perceiving them.* Prince Hjalmar.

It rains; there is a burial in the graveyard. They have dug two graves, and the *dies tree* comes into the house. There is not a window but looks out on the graveyard; it eats into the very gardens of the castle; and the last graves come down as far as the pond. They are opening the coffin; I shall close the window.

ANNE.

My lord!

HJALMAR.

Ha! I did not see you.

ANNE.

We have just come in.

HJALMAR.

Ah f ANNE.

What were you thinking of, my lord?
. HJALMAR.

Of nothing, madam.

ANNE.

Of nothing? At the end of the month, my lord,...

HJALMAR.

At the end of the month, madam?

ANNE.

Your happy wedding-day.

HJALMAR.

Yes, madam.

ANNE.

Why do you come no nearer, my lord?

KING.

Ay, come nearer, Hjalmar.

ANNE.

Why is it you are so cold, my lord? Are you afraid of me? Yet you are almost my son; and I love you like a mother, — perhaps more than a mother. Give me

your hand, HJALMAR.

My hand, madam?

ANNE.

Yes, your hand; and look into my eyes. Do you not see there that I love you? You have never kissed me — to this day.

HJALMAR.

Kiss you, madam?

ANNE.

Ay, kiss me; did you not kiss your mother? I would kiss you every day. — I dreamt of you last night.

HJALMAR.

Of me, madam?

ANNE.

Yes, of you. I will tell you my dream some day. — Your hand is quite cold, and your cheeks are burning. Give me your other hand.

HJALMAR.

My other hand?

ANNE.

Yes. It is cold, too, and pale as a hand of snow. I would warm those hands again. — Aie you ill?

HJALMAR.

Yes, madam.

ANNE.

Our love will heal you. *Exeunt.* Scene III.—*A street in the village.*

Enter Princess Maleine *and* Nurse.

MALEINE.

Leaning over the parapet of a bridge. I do not know myself any longer when I look in the water. NURSE.

Fasten your cloak; the gold fringe of your gown can be seen, — some peasants are coming.

Enter two old Peasants. FIRST PEASANT.

There's the girl.

SECOND PEASANT.

The one who came to-day?

FIRST PEASANT.

Yes; with an old woman.

SECOND PEASANT.

Where does she come from?

FIRST PEASANT.

Nobody knows, SECOND PEASANT.

That does not speak well for her.

FIRST PEASANT.

She's the talk of the whole village.

SECOND PEASANT.

There's nothing extraordinary about her, all the same.

FIRST PEASANT.

She's thin.

SECOND PEASANT.

Where is she living?

FIRST PEASANT.

At the Blue Lion.

SECOND PEASANT.

Has she money?

FIRST PEASANT.

They say so.

SECOND PEASANT.

We must see. *Exeunt. Enter a* Cowherd.

COWHERD.

Good-evening!

MALEINE AND NURSE.

Good-evening!

COWHERD.

Fine weather to-night.

NURSE.

Yes, rather fine.

COWHERD.

Thanks to the moon.

NURSE.

Yes.

COWHERD.

But it was hot during the day.

NURSE.

Oh! yes, it *was* hot during the day.

COWHERD. *Going down towards the water.*, I am going to bathe. NURSE.

To bathe?

COWHERD.

Yes; I am going to undress here.

NURSE.

To undress in our presence?

COWHERD.

Yes, NURSE.

To Maleine. Come away! COWHERD.

Have you never seen a man stark naked?

Enter, running, an Old Woman, *in tears. She begins screaming at the door of the Blue Lion Inn.* OLD WOMAN.

Help! Help! My God! My God! Open the door, quick! They 're murdering each other with big carving-knives.

TIPPLERS. *Opening the door.* What is the matter? OLD WOMAN.

My son! My poor son! They 're murdering each other with big knives! With big carving-knives!

VOICES FROM THE WINDOWS.

What's the matter?

TIPPLERS.

A fight!

VOICES FROM THE WTNDOWS.
Oh, we are coming down to see!
TIPPLERS.
Where are they?
OLD WOMAN.
Behind the Golden Star; he is fighting with the blacksmith about that girl who came to the village to-day; they are both bleeding already!
TIPPLERS.
Both bleeding already?
OLD WOMAN.
There's blood on the walls, already.
SOME.
There's blood on the walls, already?
OTHERS.
Let us go and look. Where are they?
OLD WOMAN.
Behind the Golden Star. You can see them from here.
TIPPLERS.
You can see them from here? — With big carving-knives? — How they must be bleeding! — Look out, there! the Prince!

They re-enter the Blue Lion, dragging in the Old Woman, who screams and struggles *Enter* Prince Hjalmar *and* Angus. MALEINE.
To Nurse. Hjalmar! NURSE.
Hide yourself.
Exeunt Maleine *and* Nurse ANGUS.
Did you see that little peasant girl?
HJALMAR.
A glimpse... a mere glimpse.
ANGUS.
She looks strange.
HJALMAR.
I do not like her.
ANGUS.
I find her admirable myself, and I shall mention her to Princess Uglyane; she needs a maid-servant. Oh, how pale you are!
HJALMAR.
Am I pale?
ANGUS.
Wonderfully pale. Are you ill?
HJALMAR.
No. It is the strange heat of this autumn day. I have felt all day as if I were living in a room full of the fever-stricken; and now this night, cold as a cellar! I have not gone outside the castle to-day, and the damp of the night took hold on me

in the avenue.
ANGUS.
Be careful! There are many sick in the village.
HJALMAR.'
Yes, it is the marshes; and behold, I am in the midst of marshes myself.
ANGUS.
What?
HJALMAR.
I saw almost to-day the flame of sins to which as yet I dare not give a name.
ANGUS.
I do not understand you.
HJALMAR.
No more did I understand certain words of Queen Anne. I am afraid to understand them.
ANGUS.
What has happened to-day?
HJALMAR.
A little thing; but I am afraid of what I shall see beyond my wedding-day. Oh! oh! look yonder, Angus!
Here the King and Queen Anne are seen kissing at one of the windows of the castle ANGUS.
Beware; do not look; they will see us.
HJALMAR.
No; we are in darkness, and their room is lighted. But look, how red the sky has grown over the castle.
ANGUS.
There will be a storm to-morrow.
HJALMAR.
And yet she does not love him....
ANGUS.
Let us go.
HJALMAR.
I dare not look any longer at that sky. God knows what colors it has taken over our heads to-day. You do not know what I beheld this afternoon in that castle, where I believe the very stones are poisonous, where the touch of Queen Anne's hands made me sweat more than the September sun on the walls.
ANGUS.
'Oh, what has happened?
HJALMAR.
Let us not speak of it any more. — Where is that little peasant girl?
Outcries from within the Blue Lion. ANGUS.
What is that?

HJALMAR.
I do not know. There has been a strange unrest in the village all the afternoon. Let us go. You will understand some day what I have said. _*Exeunt.*
A TIPPLER.
Opening the inn-door.. He has gone!
ALL THE TIPPLERS. *On the threshold.* He has gone. — Now, we may go and see. — How they must be bleeding! — Perhaps they are dead. *Exeunt.*
Scene IV. — *An apartment in the castle.*
Queen Anne, Princess Uglyane, Princess Maleine, *dressed as a maid-servant, and another maid-servant discovered.* ANNE.
Bring another cloak. — I think the green one will go better.
UGLYANE.
I do not want it. — A peacock-green velvet cloak over a sea-green gown!
ANNE.
I don't know...
UGLYANE.
"/ don't know! I don't know!" You never know, when others are concerned!
ANNE.
Come, don't get in a temper. I meant well in suggesting it. You will be scarlet when you get to the trysting-place.
UGLYANE.
I shall be scarlet when I get to the trysting-place! Oh, it is enough to make one throw one's self out of the window. You don't know what to imagine next to torment me!
ANNE.
Uglyane! Uglyane! Come, come. — Bring another cloak.
MAID-SERVANT.
This one, madam?
S ANNE.
Yes, — turn round. Yes, this is infinitely better.
UGLYANE.
And my hair! — so?
ANNE.
It should be smoothed a little more on the forehead.
UGLYANE.
Where is my mirror?
ANNE.
Where is her mirror? *To* Maleine. You are not doing anything! Bring her mirror! — She has been here a week, and

she will never know anything. — Have you come from the moon? — Come now, make haste. Where are you?

MALEINE.

Here, madam.

UGLYANE.

Now, do not incline that mirror so! — I can see all the weeping willows of the garden in it; they seem to be weeping over your face.

ANNE.

Yes, so, — but let them flow down her back.

— Unfortunately, it will be too dark in the wood....

UGLYANE.

It will be dark?

ANNE.

He will not see you — there are great clouds across the moon.

i UGLYANE.

But why does he wish me to come to the garden? If it were in July, or even by daylight,

— but at night, in the fall of the year! It is cold! raining! windy! Shall I wear any jewels?

ANNE.

Of course. — But we are going — *Whispers in her ear.* UGLYANE.

Yes.

ANNE. *To* Maleine *and the other maid-servant.* You may go; and do not return until you are called for. *Exeunt* Princess Maleine *and other maid-servant.*

Scene V. — *A corridor in the castle. Enter* Princess Maleine. — *She goes to a door at the end of the passage and knocks.*

Anne *(within).* Who's there?

MALEINE.

I.

ANNE.

Who are you?

MALEINE.

Princess Ma. . the new maid-servant.

ANNE. *Partly opening the doorj* What do you want here? MALEINE.

I have come on an errand from...

ANNE.

Do not come in. Well?

MALEINE.

I have come on an errand from Prince Hjalmar.

ANNE.

Yes, yes! She is coming! she is coming. In one minute! It is not yet eight. Leave us. MALEINE.

An officer told me that he was away.

ANNE.

Who was away?

MALEINE.

Prince Hjalmar.

ANNE.

Prince Hjalmar is away?

MALEINE.

He has left the castle.

ANNE.

Where has he gone?

UGLYANE. *Within.* What is the matter?

ANNE.

The Prince has left the castle.

UGLYANE. /» *the doorway.* What? ANNE. The prince has left the castle!

MALEINE.

Yes.

UGLYANE.

Impossible!

ANNE.

Where has he gone?

MALEINE.

I do not know. I think he went toward the forest; and he sends word that he will not be able to come to the tryst.

ANNE.

Who told you so?

MALEINE.

An officer.

ANNE.

What officer?

MALEINE.

I do not know his name........

ANNE.

Where is this officer?

MALEINE.

He went away with the Prince.

ANNE.

Why did n't he come here himself?

MALEINE.

I told him you wished to be alone.

ANNE.

Who told you to say that? My God! What can have happened? Go away!

Door closes. Exit Maleine.

Scene VI. — *A wood within a park.*

HJALMAR.

She told me to await her by the fountain. I have a wish to see her in the dusk. ... I would see if the night will give her pause. — Will she not have a little si-

lence in her heart? — I never saw the autumn wood more weird than to-night. I never saw the wood darker than to-night. By what light shall we see each other? I cannot make out my own hands. — But what are all those points of light about me? Have all the owls in the park come here? Away! Away! To the graveyard! back to the dead! *Throws earth at them.* Are you the guests for a wedding night? Here I am with hands like a grave-digger's now! — Oh, I shall not come back here very often! — Hark, she is coming!

— Is it the wind? — Oh! how the leaves are falling about me now! There is a tree that is absolutely stripped. And how the clouds fidget across the moon! — Ah! these are weepingwillow leaves that are falling so on my hands.

— Oh! I should not have come hither! — I never saw the wood more grewsome than tonight. — I never saw so many ill omens as to-night. — She comes!

Enter Princess Maleine. MALEINE.

Where are you, my lord?

HJALMAR.

Here.

MALEINE.

But where? — I cannot see.

HJALMAR.

Here, by the fountain. — We shall see each other by the light of the water. It is uncanny here this evening.

MALEINE.

Yes, — I am afraid! — ah! I have found you.

HJALMAR.

Why are you trembling?

MALEINE.

I am not trembling.

HJALMAR.

I cannot see you; come this way, there is more light here; and throw back your head a little to the sky. — You too look weird to-night. — One would say my eyes had just opened tonight. — One would say my heart was opening to-night. — Indeed, I believe you are really beautiful. — Oh, you are strangely beautiful, Uglyane! — I think I must never have looked at you until now. — Oh, I think you are strangely beautiful. — There is something about you this evening.... Let us go somewhere else, in the light. — Come!

MALEINE.
Not yet.

HJALMAR.
Uglyane! Uglyane!

Kisses her; the fountain, agitated by the wind, collapses and splashes them.

MALEINE.
Oh! What have you done?

HJALMAR.
It is the fountain.

MALEINE.
Oh! Oh!

HJALMAR.
It is the wind.

MALEINE.
I am afraid.

HJALMAR.
Do not think of that any longer. Let us go further away. Let us not think of that any more. Oh! Oh! Oh! I am wet all over.

MALEINE.
There is some one weeping here.

HJALMAR.
Some one weeping here?

MALEINE.
I am afraid.

HJALMAR.
Listen; it is the wind.

MALEINE.
But what are all those eyes up in the trees?

HJALMAR.
Where? Oh, those are the owls. They have come back. I will drive them away. *Throws earth at them.* Away! Away!

MALEINE.
There is one of them that will not go.

HJALMAR.
Where is it?

MALEINE.
On the weeping willow.

HJALMAR.
Away!

MALEINE.
He does not move.

HJALMAR.
Away! Away! *Throws earth: tM $wl.*

MALEINE.
Oh! you have thrown earth on me.

HJALMAR.
I have thrown earth on you?

MALEINE.

Yes; it fell back on me.

HJALMAR.
Oh, my poor Uglyane!

MALEINE.
I am afraid.

HJALMAR.
Afraid — at my side?

MALEINE.
There are flames there between the trees.

HJALMAR.
It is nothing, — it is summer lightning; it has been very sultry to-day.

MALEINE.
I am afraid. Oh! who is moving the earth about us?

HJALMAR.
It is nothing; it is a mole, — a poor little mole at work.

MALEINE.
I am afraid....

HJALMAR.
But we are within the park here.

MALEINE.
Are there walls about the park?

HJALMAR.
Of course; there are walls and ditches about the park.

MALEINE.
And can nobody enter?

HJALMAR.
No, — but there are many unknown things that enter, in spite of all.

MALEINE.
My nose is bleeding.

HJALMAR.
Your nose is bleeding?

MALEINE.
Yes. Where is my handkerchief?

HJALMAR.
Let us go to the basin.

MALEINE.
Oh! my gown is all stained with blood already.

HJALMAR.
Uglyane! Uglyane! Has it stopped?

A pause. MALEINE.
Yes.

HJALMAR.
What are you thinking of?

MALEINE.
I am sad.

HJALMAR.
You are sad? What are you thinking of, Uglyane?

1 MALEINE.
I am thinking of Princess Maleine.

HJALMAR.
What did you say?

MALEINE.
I am thinking of Princess Maleine.

HJALMAR.
Do you know Princess Maleine?

MALEINE.
I am Princess Maleine.

HJALMAR.
What?

MALEINE.
I am Princess Maleine.

HJALMAR.
You are not Uglyane?

MALEINE.
I am Princess Maleine.

HJALMAR.
You are Princess Maleine? You are Princess Maleine? But she is dead!

MALEINE.
I am Princess Maleine.

The moon comes out between the trees, and reveals Princess Maleine.

HJALMAR.
Oh, Maleine! — Whence come you? And how have you come so far? How can you have come so far?

MALEINE.
I do not know.

HJALMAR.
O God! O God! O God! O God! What have I escaped to-day! What a stone you have rolled away this night! O God! From what tomb have I risen this evening!— Maleine! Maleine! What shall we do now? — Maleine!... I believe I am in heaven, up to the heart!...

MALEINE.
Oh! and so do I.

The fountain sobs strangely and expires BOTH.

Turning round., Oh! MALEINE.
What can it be? What can it be now?

HJALMAR.
Do not weep; do not be afraid. It is the fountain.

MALEINE.
What is happening here? What is going to happen? Let me go away! Let me go away! Let me go away!

HJALMAR.
Do not weep.

MALEINE.

Take me away.

HJALMAR *(looking, toward the fountain).*

It is dead; let us go somewhere else.

Exeunt. curtain. ACT THIRD.

Scene I. — *An apartment in the castle.*
The King. *Enter* Prince Hjalmar.

HJALMAR.

Father?

KING.

Hjalmar!

HJALMAR.

I wish to speak to you, father.

KING.

What do you wish to speak to me about?

HJALMAR.

Are you ill, father?

KING.

Yes, I am ill; and see how old I am getting. My hair has almost all fallen out. See how my hands shake now; and I feel as though I had all the fires of hell in my head.

HJALMAR.

Father! My poor father! You should go away, — somewhere else, perhaps, — I do not know....

KING.

I cannot go away! — Why have you come here? I am expecting somebody.

HJALMAR.

I wished to speak to you.

KING.

Of what?

HJALMAR.

Of Princess Maleine.

KING.

Of what? — I can hardly hear any more.

HJALMAR.

Of Princess Maleine. Princess Maleine has come back.

KING.

Princess Maleine has come back!

HJALMAR.

Yes.

KING.

But she is dead!

HJALMAR.

She has come back.

KING.

But she is dead — I saw her.

HJALMAR.

She has come back.

KING.

Where is she?

HJALMAR.

Here.

KING.

Here, in the castle?

HJALMAR.

Yes.

KING.

Show her to me; I would like to see her!

HJALMAR.

Not yet. — Father, I can no longer espouse Uglyane.

KING.

You can no longer espouse Uglyane?

HJALMAR.

I never loved any one but Princess Maleine.

KING.

It is impossible, Hjalmar! — Hjalmar! — Besides, she will go away.

HJALMAR.

Who?

KING.

Anne.

HJALMAR.

It must be broken to her gradually.

KING.

I?—I break it to her? — Hark!... I think she is coming up the staircase. My God! — My God! What will happen? — Hjalmar, wait!... *Exit.* HJALMAR.

Father! My poor father! — She will kill him before the month is ended.

Re-enter King.

King.

Do not let her know yet — not to-day. *Exit.* HJALMAR.

My God! My God! — I think I hear him in the oratory. — She is coming here. — For some days she has followed me like my shadow. *Enter* Queen Anne. Good-evening, madam.

ANNE.

Oh! it is you, Hjalmar. — I did not expect...

HJALMAR. I wished to speak to you, madam. ANNE.

You have never had anything to say to me.,,, Are we alone?

HJALMAR.

Yes, madam.

ANNE.

Then come here by me. Sit here by me.

HJALMAR.

But one word, madam. — Did you ever hear of Princess Maleine?

ANNE.

Of Princess Maleine?

HJALMAR.

Yes, madam.

ANNE.

Yes, Hjalmar; — but she is dead.

HJALMAR.

They say she lives, perhaps.

ANNE.

But it was the king himself who slew her.

HJALMAR.

They say she lives, perhaps.

ANNE.

So much the better for her.

HJALMAR.

Perhaps you will see her, ANNE.

Oh! Oh! Oh! In the next world, you mean?

HJALMAR.

Oh! *Exit.* ANNE.

Where are you going, my lord? And why do you flee from me? — Why do you flee from me? *Exit.*

Scene II. — *A festal hall in the castle.*
King, Queen Anne, Hjalmar, Uglyane, Angus, Maids-of-honor, Lords, Etc. *Dancing. Music.* ANNE.

Come here by me, my lord; you seem transfigured to-night.

HJALMAR.

Is not my betrothed at my side?

ANNE.

Let me put my hand on your heart a moment. Oh! It beats its wings already as if it would fly away toward I know not what heaven.

HJALMAR.

Your hand alone retains it, madam.

ANNE.

I do not understand.... I do not understand. You will explain that to me later. *To the* King. You are sad, my lord; what are you thinking of?

KING.

I? — I am not sad; but I am getting very old.

ANNE.

Come, do not speak so on a gala night! Admire your son, rather. Is he not admirable in that black and violet stlk doublet? And have I not chosen a handsome spouse for my daughter?

HJALMAR.

Madam, I am going away to join Angus. He will throw a little water on the fire, whereas you only pour oil on it.

ANNE.

Do not return drenched by the rain of his fine speeches...

HJALMAR.

They will fall in broad sunlight!

ANGUS.

Hjalmar! Hjalmar HJALMAR.

Oh, I know what you are going to say; but this has nothing to do with what you think.

ANGUS.

You are no longer yourself to-day. What happened to you yesterday evening?

HJALMAR.

Yesterday evening? — Oh, strange things happened yesterday evening. — But I would rather not speak of them at present. Go some night into the wood in the park, near the fountain; and you will notice that it is only at certain times and when you are looking at them, that things keep still like good children and do not seem strange and wild; but as soon as your back is turned on them, they begin making faces at you, and playing naughty tricks.

ANGUS.

I do not understand.

HJALMAR.

No more do I; but I would rather live among men, — were they all against me.

ANGUS.

What?

HJALMAR.

Po pot go away far!

ANGUS.

Why?

HJALMAR.

I do not know yet.

ANNE.

Will you soon have done, my lord? One does not abandon his betrothed so....

HJALMAR.

I fly, madam. *To* Uglyane. Angus has just told me of a strange adventure, Uglyane.

UGLYANE.

Really?

HJALMAR.

Yes, — it is about a young girl; a poor young girl who lost all the money she had.

UGLYANE.

Oh!

HJALMAR.

Yes! she has lost all her money.... And she wishes to marry him, in spite of all. She waits for him in the garden every evening; she pursues him in the moonlight; he has no longer a moment's rest.

UGLYANE.

What is he going to do?

HJALMAR.

He does not know at all. I told him to have the drawbridges raised, and place a man-at-arms at every door, so that she may not enter again. But he will not.

UGLYANE.

Why?

HJALMAR.

I don't know at all. — Oh! my dear Uglyane!

ANGUS. *To* Hjalmar. Do you not shiver as you pass into the ice-caverns of marriage? HJALMAR.

We shall make them caverns of flame.

KING. *In a loud voice.* I cannot see any dancing at all from here. ANNE.

But you are not three steps from the dancers, my lord.

KING.

I thought I was far away from them.

ANGUS. *To* Hjalmar. Have you noticed how pale and weary your father has been looking for some time? HJALMAR.

Yes, yes....

ANGUS.

He has grown strangely old of late.

KING. *In a loud voice."* I believe death is beginning to knock at my door.

All shudder. A pause. Music suddenly ceases. Knocking at the door.

ANNE.

Some one is knocking at the little door.

HJALMAR.

Come in!

The door opens, partly revealing Princess

Maleine in long white bridal robes.

ANNE.

Who comes?

HJALMAR.

Princess Maleine!

ANNE.

Who?

HJALMAR.

Princess Maleine!

KING.

Close the door!

ALL.

Close the door!

HJALMAR.

Why close the door? king *swoons.* AN-GUS.

Help! Help! The King is fainting.

A MAID OF HONOR.

Go get a glass of water.

HJALMAR.

Father! — Help me!...

ANOTHER MAID OF HONOR.

Go get a priest!

A LORD.

Open the windows!

ANGUS.

Stand back! Stand back!

HJALMAR.

Call a physician. Let us carry him to his bed. Help me.

ANGUS.

There is a strange storm about the castle to-night. *Exeunt. Scene* III. — *Before the castle. Enter the* King *and* Queen Anne,

King.

But perhaps we could send the little maid away?

ANNE.

And meet her again to-morrow? Or must we wait for a sea of troubles; must we wait until Hjalmar rejoin her? Must we...

KING.

My God! My God! What do you want me to do?

ANNE.

You will do what you please; but you must choose between that girl and me.

KING.

You never know what he thinks....

ANNE.

I am sure he does not love her. He thought her dead. Did you see one tear roll down upon his cheeks?

KING. , They do not always roll down the cheeks. ANNE.

He would not have thrown himself into Uglyane's arms.

KING.

Wait a few days. — He might die of it...
..

ANNE.

We will wait. — He will not notice.

KING.

I have no other child....

ANNE.

The more reason you should make him happy. — Beware, now! Here he comes with his waxen beggar girl; he has been taking her for a walk round the marshes, and the night air has already made her greener than if she had been drowned these four weeks. *Enter* Prince Hjalmar *and* Princess Maleine. Good-evening, Hjalmar! — Good-evening, Maleine! You have taken a little walk.

HJALMAR.

Yes, madam.

ANNE.

It would be better, though, not to go out in the evening. Maleine must be careful. She seems to me a little pale, already. The air of the marshes is very injurious.

MALEINE.

So I have been told, madam.

ANNE.

Oh! it is downright poison!

HJALMAR.

We had not been out all day, and the moonlight enticed us; we have been to look at the windmills along the canal.

ANNE.

You should be careful at first; I was sick myself.

KING.

Every one is sick on arriving here.

HJALMAR.

There are many sick in the village.

KING.

And many dead in the graveyard.

ANNE.

Come, come; do not frighten this child. *Enter* The Madman.

HJALMAR.

Maleine, the madman 1 MALEINE.

Oh!

ANNE.

Have you not seen him before, Maleine? Don't be afraid, don't be afraid; he is harmless. He wanders about like this every evening.

HJALMAR.

Every night he goes digging graves in the orchard.

MALEINE.

Why?

HJALMAR.

No one knows.

MALEINE.

Is he pointing at me with his finger?

HJALMAR.

Yes; pay no attention to him.

MALEINE.

He is making the sign of the cross.

THE MADMAN.

Oh! Oh! Oh!

MALEINE.

I am afraid.

HJALMAR.

He has a frightened look.

THE MADMAN.

Oh! Oh! Oh!

HJALMAR.

He is going away. *Exit* The Madman.

ANNE.

When will the wedding be, Maleine?

HJALMAR.

Before the end of the month, if my father will consent.

KING.

Yes, yes....

ANNE.

You know I remain here until your wedding; and so does Uglyane! Oh! poor Uglyane! Hjalmar, Hjalmar, how you have deserted her!

HJALMAR.

Madam!...

ANNE.

Oh! you need have no remorse; it is better to tell you at once. She was obeying her father more than her heart. She was fond of you, though; but what would you have? She was brought up and passed her whole childhood with her cousin, Prince Osric, and such things are not forgotten. She cried all the tears in her poor little heart when she took leave of him; and I had to drag her here.

MALEINE.

There is something black coming.

KING.

Whom do you mean?

HJALMAR.

What?

MALEINE.

There is something black coming.

HJALMAR.

Where?

MALEINE.

Yonder; in the fog, by the graveyard.

HJALMAR.

Oh! that is the seven nuns.

MALEINE.

Seven nuns!

ANNE.

Yes! They are coming to spin for your wedding. *Enter* Nurse *and the* Seven Nuns.

NURSE.

Good-evening!   Good-evening, Maleine!

SEVEN NUNS.

Good-evening!

ALL.

Good-evening, sisters.

MALEINE.

Oh! what is she carrying?

HJALMAR.

Who?

MALEINE.

The third one; the oldest?

NURSE.

It is linen for you, Maleine.

Exeunt Seven Nuns. *A chunk bell rings without.* HJALMAR.

The bell is ringing for vespers. — Come, Maleine.

MALEINE.

I am cold.

HJALMAR.

You are pale, let us go in.

MALEINE.

Oh! what a number of crows there are around us. *Croakings.* HJALMAR.

Come in!

MALEINE.

What are all those flames over the marshes? Will-o'-the-wisps are seen over the marshes.

NURSE.

They say they are souls.

HJALMAR.

They are will-o'-the-wisps. — Come!

MALEINE.

Oh! there is a long one going toward the graveyard.

HJALMAR.

Come! Come!

KING.

I shall go in, too. Anne, are you coming?

ANNE.

I follow you. *Exeunt* King, Hjalmar *and* Maleine. Maleine appears rather unwell. She must be taken care of.

Nurse.

She is a little pale, madam. But she is

not ill. She is stronger than you think.

ANNE.

I should not be astonished if she fell sick.

Exit with Nurse. Scene IV. — *A room in the* Physician's *house. Enter the* Physician, Physician.

She has asked me for poison. There is a mystery over the castle, and I believe its walls will fall upon our heads. And woe to the little ones in the house! There are already strange rumors in the air, and it seems to me that on the other side of this world they are beginning to be a little uneasy about adultery. Meanwhile, the people here wade in misery up to their lips; and the old King will die in the Queen's bed before the end of the month.... He has been growing strangely white for several weeks; and his mind begins to totter, as well as his body. I must not be caught in the midst of the storms that are coming. It is time I should be gone; it is time I should be gone! I have no desire to go blindly with her into that hell! I must give her some almost harmless poison to deceive her; but I shall break silence before they close a tomb. Meanwhile I wash my hands of it. I will not be killed trying to hold up a crumbling tower!

Exit.

Scene V. — *A courtyard in the castle, Enter* King,

King.

My God! My God! Would I were elsewhere! Would I might sleep until the month were ended! I should be glad to die! She leads me like a poor spaniel; she is going to drag me into a forest of crimes, and the flames of hell are about my path. My God! If I could but retrace my steps! Was there no way to send the little maid out of the country? I wept this morning when I saw her ill. Could she but leave this poisonous castle! I want to go away, no matter where! No matter where! Would I might see the towers crumble into the pool. I fancy everything I eat is poisoned; and the very sky looks poisonous to-night. But, my God! the poison in that poor little white body. Oh! Oh! Oh! *Enter* Queen Anne. They are coming?

ANNE.

Yes; they are coming.

KING.

I am going away.

    What?

ANNE. KING.

I am going away;. I cannot look upon it any longer.

ANNE.

What is that? You are going to stay. Sit there! Don't look so strange.

KING.

Do I look strange?

ANNE.

Yes, they will observe it. Try to look happy.

KING.

Oh! Oh! Happy!

ANNE.

Now, then; be silent. They are here!

KING.

My God! My God! How pale she is!

Enter Prince Hjalmar, Maleine, *and* Little Allan.

ANNE.

Well, Maleine, how do you feel?

MALEINE.

A little better; a little better.

ANNE.

You look brighter; sit down here, Maleine; I have had cushions brought; the air is very pure this evening.

KING.

The stars are out.

ANNE.

I do not see any.

KING.

I thought I saw some over there.

ANNE.

Where are your wits?

KING.

I do not know.

ANNE.

Are you comfortable, Maleine?

MALEINE.

Yes, yes.

ANNE.

Are you tired?

MALEINE.

A little, madam.

ANNE.

Let me put this cushion under your elbow.

MALEINE.

Thank you, madam.

HJALMAR.

She is so patient.. Oh! my poor Maleine!

ANNE.

Come, come; it is nothing. You must take courage. It is the air of the marshes. Uglyane is sick, too.

HJALMAR.

Uglyane is sick?

ANNE.

She is sick, like Maleine; she no longer leaves her room.

KING.

Maleine would do better to'leave the castle.

ANNE.

What?

KING.

I was saying that Maleine would do better, perhaps, to go elsewhere....

HJALMAR.

I have said so as well.

ANNE.

Where would she go?

KING.

I do not know.

ANNE.

No, no; it is better she should remain here; she will get used to the air of the marshes. Good heavens, I have been sick myself. Where would she be better nursed than here? Is it not best she should remain here?

KING.

Oh! Oh!

ANNE.

What?

KING.

Yes! Yes!

ANNE.

Good! — Well, well, Allan; what's the matter? Why do you stare at us so, child? Come, kiss me; now go and play with your ball.

LITTLE ALLAN.

Is Ma-a-leine si-ick?

ANNE.

Yes, a litfle.

LITTLE ALLAN.

Very, very, ve-ry si-ick?

ANNE.

No, no.

LITTLE ALLAN.

Wo-on't she play with me any mo-ore?

ANNE.

Yes, yes, she will play with you again;

will you not, Maleine?

LITTLE ALLAN.

Oh! the wi-indmill has sto-opped!

ANNE.

What?

LITTLE ALLAN.

The wi-indmill has sto-opped!

ANNE.

What windmill?

LITTLE ALLAN.

The-ere; the black wi-indmill!

ANNE.

Well, that is because the miller has gone to bed.

LITTLE ALLAN.

I-is he si-ick?

ANNE.

I do not know! Now, then, be quiet; go and play.

LITTLE ALLAN.

Why is Ma-a-leine shutting her eyes?

ANNE.

She is tired.

LITTLE ALLAN.

O-open your eyes, Ma-a-leine!

ANNE.

Now, will you leave us in quiet; go and play....

LITTLE ALLAN.

O-pen your eyes, Ma-a-leine!

ANNE.

Go and play; go and play. Ah, you have put on your black velvet mantle, Maleine.

MALEINE.

Yes, madam.

HJALMAR.

It is rather melancholy.

ANNE.

It is admirable. *To the* King. Have you noticed it, my lord?

KING.

I?

ANNE.

Yes, you?

KING.

What?

ANNE.

Where are your wits? I am speaking of the black velvet mantle.

KING.

I see a cypress yonder making signs to me.

ALL.

What?

KING.

I see a cypress yonder making signs to me.

ANNE.

Have you fallen asleep? Are you dreaming?

KING.

I?

ANNE.

I was speaking of the black velvet mantle.

KING.

Oh! — Yes, it is very beautiful....

ANNE.

Oh! Oh! Oh! he had fallen asleep.— How do you feel, Maleine?

MALEINE.

Better, better.

KING.

No, no! It is too horrible.

HJALMAR.

What is the matter?

ANNE.

What is so horrible now?

KING.

Nothing! nothing!

ANNE.

Be careful what you say. You are frightening everybody.

KING.

I? Frightening everybody?

ANNE.

Oh! please do not be forever repeating what we say! What is the matter with you to-night? Are you ill?

HJALMAR.

You are sleepy, father?

KING.

No, no; I am not sleepy!

ANNE.

What are you thinking about?

KING.

Maleine?

MALEINE.

Sire?

KING.

I have never yet kissed you, have I?

MALEINE.

No, sire.

KING.

May I kiss you to-night?

MALEINE.

Certainly, sire.

KING. *Kissing her.'* Oh, Maleine! Maleine! MALEINE.

Sire? — what troubles you?

KING.

My hair is turning white, you see.

MALEINE.

Do you love me a little to-day?

KING.

Oh, yes, Maleine!... Give me your little hand! — Oh! oh! It is still as hot as a little fire....

MALEINE.

What can be troubling him? Now what *can* be the matter?

ANNE.

Come, come. You are making her cry.

KING.

I would that I were dead!

ANNE.

Pray, do not say any more such things tonight.

HJALMAR.

Let us be gone!

Here a strange knock is heard at the gates.

ANNE.

Some one is knocking.

HJALMAR.

Who can be knocking at this hour?

ANNE.

No one answers. *Another knock.* KING.

Who can it be?

HJALMAR.

Knock a little louder; they do not hear you.

ANNE.

They do not open the gates so late.

HJALMAR.

They do not open the gates so late. Come back to-morrow. *Another ktwck.*

King. « Oh! Oh! Oh! *Another knock.*

ANNE.

What can they be knocking with?

HJALMAR.

I do not know.

ANNE.

Go and look.

HJALMAR.

I will. *Opens the gate.* ANNE.

Who is it?

HJALMAR.

I do not know. I can't see very well.

ANNE.

Come in!

MALEINE.

I am cold.

HJALMAR.

There is no one here.

ALL.

There is no one there?

HJALMAR.

It is dark; I see no one.

ANNE.

Then it is the wind; it must be the wind.

HJALMAR.

Yes, I think it is the cypress.

KING.

Oh!

ANNE.

Would it not be best for us to go in?

HJALMAR.

Yes. _Exeunt. ACT FOURTH.

Scene I. — *In the gardens. Enter* Hjalmar. HJALMAR.

She has been following me like a dog of late. She was at one of the windows of the tower; she saw me cross the bridge in the garden, and here she comes, at the end of the walk. — I shall go away. *Exit. Enter* Queen Anne. ANNE.

He avoids me of late. I fear his suspicions are aroused. I will not wait any longer. That poison will drag along till the Day of Judgment. I can no longer trust anybody; I think the King is going mad. I have to keep him constantly under my eyes. He keeps wandering about Maleine's chamber, and I believe he wants to give her warning. — I have taken the key of that room away. It is time to make an end of it. — Ah! Here is the nurse! She is always with the girl. She must be sent away to-day. Good-morning, nurse.

Enter Nurse. NURSE.

Good-morning, good-morning, madam.

ANNE.

Fine weather, is it not, nurse?

NURSE.

Yes, madam; rather warm, though, — rather warm for this time of the year.

ANNE.

These are the last of the sunny days; we must enjoy them.

NURSE.

I have no longer had time to come into the garden since Maleine has been ill.

ANNE.

Is she better?

NURSE.

Yes; a little better perhaps; but weak, so weak always, and pale, so pale!

ANNE.

I saw the physician this morning; he told me that, above all, she needed rest.

NURSE.

So he told me.

ANNE.

He even advises that she should be left alone, and that no one go into her room, unless she calls.

NURSE.

He said nothing of the kind to me.

ANNE.

He must have forgotten; perhaps they did not dare tell you, for fear of giving you pain.

NURSE.

He was wrong; he was wrong.

ANNE.

Yes, he was wrong.

NURSE.

I have just gathered a few bunches of grapes for her.

ANNE.

Are there grapes already?

NURSE.

Yes; I found some along the wall. She likes them so much....

ANNE.

They look very fine.

NURSE.

I intended to give them to her after mass j but I will wait until she is well, ANNE.

You will not have to wait long.

Church bell sounds. NURSE.

Good heavens, they are ringing for mass! I nearly forgot it was Sunday.

ANNE.

I am going to mass myself. *Exeunt.*

Scene II. — *A kitchen in the castle.*

Maids, Cooks, Servants, *etc.* — *The Seven Nuns sit at their spinning-wheels at the farther end of the hall, chanting Latin hymns in a murmur.*

A MAN COOK.

We.are going to have a thunder storm.

A MAN-SERVANT.

I just came from the garden, and I never saw such a sky; it's as black as the pool.

A MAID-SERVANT.

Six o'clock, and I can no longer see anything. The lamps must be lighted.

ANOTHER MAID-SERVANT.

Jt j§ still as death, THIRD MAID-SERVANT.

I am afraid.

COOK.

You need not be afraid.

AN OLD WOMAN-SERVANT.

Oh, look at the sky! I am over seventy years old, and have never seen a sky like that.

A MAN-SERVANT.

Quite true.

A NUN.

Is there any holy water?

A MAID-SERVANT.

Yes, yes.

ANOTHER NUN.

Where is it?

COOK.

Wait till it thunders.

Enter a Maid-servant. MAID-SERVANT.

The Queen wishes to know whether Master Allan's supper is ready?

COOK.

Of course not; it's not yet seven. Be always sups at seven., MAID-SERVANT.

He is to sup earlier this evening.

COOK.

And why?

MAID-SERVANT.

I know nothing about it.

COOK.

Here's a pretty story. I should have been told before.

Enter a Second Maid-servant. SECOND MAID-SERVANT.

Where is Master Allan's supper?

COOK.

"Where is Master Allan's supper?" I cannot prepare his supper while you are making the sign of the cross.

SECOND MAID-SERVANT.

An egg and a little broth will do. I am to put him to bed immediately afterwards.

A MAID-SERVANT.

Is he sick?

SECOND MAID-SERVANT.

Qh. no! he is not sick, ANOTHER MAID-SERVANT.

Then, what has happened?

SECOND MAID-SERVANT.

I know nothing about it. *To the* Cook. She does not want the egg boiled,too hard.

Enter a Third Maid Servant. THIRD MAID-SERVANT.

We are not to attend the Queen to-night.
MAID-SERVANTS.
What?
THIRD MAID-SERVANT.
We are not to attend the Queen to-night. She will undress alone.
MAID-SERVANTS.
Oh! so much the better.
THIRD MAID-SERVANT.
All the lights are to be lit in her chamber.
A MAID-SERVANT.
All the lights?
THIRD MAHSERVANT,
Yes,
A MAID-SERVANT.
But why all the lights?
THIRD MAID-SERVANT.
I know nothing about it. That is her order.
ANOTHER MAID-SERVANT.
What is the matter with her to-night?
A MAN-SERVANT.
She is to meet somebody.
ANOTHER MAN-SERVANT.
The King'.
ANOTHER MAN-SERVANT.
Or Prince Hjalmar.
Enter a Fourth Maid-servant. FOURTH MAID-SERVANT.
Some water is to be carried up to the Queen's chamber.
A MAID-SERVANT.
Water? Why, there is some there.
FOURTH MAID-SERVANT.
There will npt be enough,
A MAN-SERVANT.
Is she going to bathe?
A COOK.
Are you the ones that bathe her?
A MAID-SERVANT.
Yes.
COOK.
Oh, la, la!
A MAN-SERVANT.
She is stark naked, then?
A MAID-SERVANT.
Naturally.
MAN-SERVANT.
By Jove! _A flash of lightning. ALL.
Lightning! They make the sign of the cross.
A NUN.
Do be silent, now! You will draw the lightning. You' will draw the lightning

upon us all! I shall not remain here, for one.
THE OTHER NUNS.
Nor I! Nor I! Nor I! Nor I! Nor I! Nor I!
Exeunt hurriedly, making the sign of the cross.
Scene III. — Princess Maleine's chamber.

Princess Maleine discovered stretched out upon her bed; a large black dog quivering in a corner.
MALEINE.
Here, Pluto! here, Pluto! They have left me all alone. They have left me all alone on a night like this. Hjalmar has not come to see me. My nurse has not come to see me to-day; and when I call, no one answers. Something has happened in the castle.... I have not heard a sound all day; you would think it was inhabited by the dead. — Where are you, poor old dog? Are you going to desert me, too? — Where are you, my poor Pluto? — I cannot see you in the darkness; you are as black as the room. — Is it you I see in the corner? — Oh, it is your eyes that gleam in the corner! Oh, close your eyes, for God's sake! Here, Pluto! Here, Pluto! Storm begins without. Is it you I see trembling in the corner? I never saw such trembling! He is making all the furniture tremble. — Have you seen something? — Answer me, my poor Pluto. Is anybody in the room? Come here, Pluto; come here! — Oh, come near me, upon my bed. — Indeed, you seem as though you would quiver to death in that corner. Rises and goes towards the dog, who recoils and hides under the furniture Where are you, my poor Pluto? — Oh, your eyes are on fire now. — But why are you afraid of me to-night? — I am going back to bed. Lies down again. If I could sleep a little! — My God! My God! How sick I am! And yet I do not know what it is; no one knows what it is; the physician does not know what it is; my nurse does not know what it is; Hjalmar does not know what it is.... The wind stirs the bed-curtains. Oh! some one is touching my bed-curtains. Who is touching my bed-curtains? Is anybody in my room? — There must be somebody in my room. — Oh! here is the

moonlight coming into the room. — What can that shadow be on the tapestry? — I believe the crucifix is swinging on the wall. Who is touching the crucifix? My God! My God! I cannot stay here any longer. Rises and goes to the door, which she tries to open. They have locked me in! Open the door, for the love of God! There is something in my room. — I shall die if you leave me here alone! Nurse! Nurse! Where are you? Hjalmar! Hjalmar! Hjalmar! Where are you? Returns to bed. I dare not leave my bed' again. — I shall turn toward the other side. — Then I shall not see what is there on the wall. Some white garments lying on a priedieu are slowly stirred by the wind. Oh! there is some one on the priedieu. Turns to the other side. Oh! the shadow is still on the wall. Turns back again. Oh! something is still on the priedieu. Oh! Oh! Oh! Oh! Oh! I must try to shut my eyes.
Creaking of furniture and the wind moaning. Oh! Oh! Oh! What is the matter now? There are noises in my room! Rises. I must see what is on the priedieu. — I was afraid of my wedding dress! But what is the shadow on the tapestry. Pulls the tapestry aside. It is on the wall now! Let me drink a little water. Drinks, and puts the glass down on a piece of furniture Oh! how the rushes in my room cry out! And when I walk, the whole room begins to speak. I think it is the shadow of the cypress; there is a cypress in front of my window. Goes to the window. What a gloomy room they have given me! Thunder. I can see nothing but tombstones by the flash of the lightning; and I fear lest the dead enter by the windows. Oh! what a storm in the graveyard! What a gale in the weeping willows! I am going back to bed. Lies down again. I can hear nothing more now; and the moonlight has left the room. I can hear nothing more now. I would rather hear some sound. Listens. There are footsteps in the corridor, — strange footsteps, strange footsteps!... They are whispering about my chamber; and I hear hands on the door. The dog begins to howl. Pluto! Pluto! Some one is coming in. — Pluto! Pluto! Pluto! Do not howl so! My God! My

God! I think my heart will die!

Sgene IV. — *A corridor in the castle. Enter, at the end of the corridor, the* King *and* Queen Anne. — *The* King *carries a light. The storm continues.*

ANNE.

I think the storm will be terrible to-night; there was a fearful gale in the courtyard; one of the old weeping willows has fallen into the pool.

KING.

Let us not do it.

ANNE.

What?

KING.

Is there no other way?

ANNE.

Come.

KING.

The seven nuns!

The Seven Nuns are heard coming, and singing litanies

A NUN.

In the distance. *Propitius esto!*

THE OTHER NUNS. *Farce nobis, Domine!*

A NUN.

Propitius esto! THE OTHERS. *Exaudi nos, Domine!*

A NUN.

Ab omni malo! THE OTHERS., *Libera nos, Domine!*

A NUN.

Ab omni peccato I THE OTHERS. *Libera nos, Domine!*

They enter in single file, the leader carrying a lantern, the seventh a praver-book.

A NUN., *Ab ira tua.* THE OTHERS. *Libera nos, Domine!*

A NUN.

A subitanea et improvisa morte! THE OTHERS. *Libera nos, Domine!*

A NUN.

Ab insidiis diaboli. THE OTHERS. *Libera nos, Domine!*

A NUN.

Passing before the King and Queen. *A spirita fornicationis.* THE OTHERS. *Libera nos, Domine!*

A NUN.

Ab ira et odio et omni mala votuntate. THE OTHERS. *Libera nos, Domine!*

Exeunt; their voices continue in the distance.

A NUN.

A fulgure et tempestate. THE OTHERS. *Libera nos, Domine!*

A NUN.

Far off. *A morte perpetua.* THE OTHERS.

Libera nos, Domine! ANNE.

They are gone! — Come!

KING.

Oh! let us not do it to-day!

ANNE.

Why?

KING.

It thunders so terribly!

ANNE.

Her cries will not be heard. Come!

KING.

Let us wait a little still.

ANNE.

Hush! This is the door...

KING.

Is this the door?... My God! My God! My God!

ANNE.

Where is the key?

KING.

Let us go to the end of the corridor; there may be some one there.

ANNE.

Where is the key?

KING.

Let us wait until to-morrow.

ANNE.

How is it possible? Come, the key! the key!

KING.

I believe I have forgotten it.

ANNE.

It is impossible. I gave it to you.

KING.

I cannot find it.

ANNE.

I put it in your cloak.

KING.

It is no longer there. I will go look for it.

...

ANNE.

Where?

KING.

Elsewhere.

ANNE.

No, no; stay here. You would not come back again.

KING.

Yes, yes! I will come back.

ANNE.

I shall go myself. Remain here. Where is it?

KING.

I do not know. In my bedroom....

ANNE.

But you will go away?

KING.

Oh, no; I will stay. I will stay here.

ANNE.

But you must have the key. I put it in your cloak. Look. We have no time to lose.

KING.

I cannot find it.

ANNE.

Let me see. — Here it is, of course! Now be reasonable, Hjalmar; and do not play the child to-night.... Do you no longer love me?

Would kiss him. KING. *Repelling her.*

No, no! Not now. ANNE.

Open the door!

KING.

Oh! Oh! Oh! I should be less afraid at the gate of hell! There is only a little girl behind this door; she cannot...

ANNE.

Open the door!

KING.

She cannot hold a flower in her hands! She trembles when she holds a poor little flower in her hands; and I...

ANNE.

Come, come! Do not make a scene; this is not the proper moment. — We have no time to lose!

KING.

I cannot find the keyhole.

ANNE.

Give me the light; it shakes as though the corridor were about to tumble down.

KING.

I cannot find the keyhole.

ANNE.

You are trembling?

KING.

No;... well, yes... a little. But I can no longer see anything.

ANNE.

Give me the key. *Opening the door.* Go in! *The black dog crawls out of the chamber.* KING.

There was something came out.

ANNE.

Yes.

KING.

There was something came out.

ANNE.

Be silent.

KING.

What can it be that came out of the room?

ANNE.

I do not know. — Go in; go in; go in. *They enter the chamber.*

Scene V. — Princess Maleine's *chamber.*

Princess Maleine *discovered motionless upon her bed, horror-struck and listening. Enter the* King *and* Queen Anne. *The storm increases.*

King.

I want to know what went out from the room....

ANNE.

Go on! go on!

KING.

Let me go see what went out from the room.

ANNE.

Be silent. She is there!

KING.

She is dead!— Let us be gone!

ANNE.

She is afraid.

KING.

Let us be gone! I hear her heart beat even here.

ANNE.

Go on; are you going mad?

KING.

She is looking at us. Oh! Oh!

ANNE.

Now, then! She's but a little girl! — Goodnight, Maleine. —Do you not hear me, Maleine? We come to bid you good-night. — Are you sick, Maleine? Do you not hear me? Maleine! Maleine! maleine *nods.* KING.

Oh!

ANNE.

You are terrifying! — Maleine! Maleine! Have you lost your voice?

MALEINE.

Good... night!...

ANNE.

Oh, then! you are alive still. — Have you all you need?— Let me lay aside my cloak, though. *Lays her cloak on a piece of furniture, and draws near the*

bed. Let me see. — Oh! this pillow is very hard. — Let me arrange your hair. — But why do you look at me so, Maleine? Maleine! — I have come to pet you a little. — Where is the pain? — You tremble as if you were going to die; why, you make the very bed tremble. — I have simply come to pet you a little. — Do not look at me so. One needs to be petted at your age; I will be your poor dear mamma to you. — Let me arrange your hair. —. Now, then, lift your head a little. I will tie your hair with this. — Lift your head a little. So. *Passes a cord about* Maleine's *neck.*

MALEINE.

Jumping out of bed. Oh! what have you put about my neck? ANNE.

Nothing! nothing! It is nothing. Do not scream!

MALEINE.

Ah! Ah!

ANNE.

Stop her! Stop her!

KING.

What? What?

ANNE.

She is going to scream! She is going to scream!

KING.

I cannot!...

MALEINE.

You are going to... oh! you are going to. ..

ANNE. *Seizing* Maleine. No, no! Maleine.

Mamma! Mamma! Nurse! Nurse! Hjalmar! Hjalmar! Hjalmar!

ANNE. *To* King. Where are you? KING.

Here! Here!

MALEINE. *Following* Anne *on her knees.* Wait! O! wait a little! Anne! Madam! King! King! King! Hjalmar! — Not to-day! — No, no, not now!... ANNE.

Are you going to follow me about the world on your knees? *Draws the cord tighter.* MALEINE.

Falling in the middle of the chamber? Mamma!... Oh! Oh! Oh! *The* King *goes to a seat.* ANNE.

She moves no longer. It is done already. — Where are you? Help me. She is not dead. — Are you sitting?

KING.

Yes, yes, yes!

ANNE.

Hold her feet; she is struggling. She is going to get up.

KING.

What feet? What feet? Where are they?

ANNE.

There! There! There! Pulll KING.

I cannot! I cannot!

ANNE.

But do not make her suffer needlessly! *Here the hail beats iuddenly against the windows.* KING.

Oh!

ANNE.

What have you done?

The windows! Some one is knocking at the windows!

Yes, yes! With fingers — oh! millions of KING.

ANNE.

Knocking at the windows?

KING. ANNE.

Yes; I have seen for myself. — Her eyes are glazing.

KING.

I want to go! I am going! I am going!

ANNE.

What? what? — Wait, wait! — She is dead.

Here the wind violently blows open a window, and a vase on the sill, containing a lily, falls noisily into the room. KING.

Oh, oh! — and now! — What is the matter now?

ANNE.

Nothing; it is the lily. The lily has fallen.

KING.

Some one opened the window.

ANNE.

It was the wind. *Thunder and lightning,* KING.

Was it really the wind?

ANNE.

Yes, yes; you hear it well enough. Take away the other lily. It is going to fall, too.

KING.

Where? Where?

ANNE.

There! There! In the window. It's going to fall; it is going to fall! Some one will hear it.

KING. *Taking the Uly* Where, must I put

it? Where must I put it? ANNE.

Where you choose, of course. On the floor; on the floor.

KING.

I do not know where; I do not know where....

ANNE.

Now, do not stand there with the lily in your hands. It shakes as if it were in the midst of a storm! It is going to fall!

KING.

Where must I put it?

ANNE.

Where you choose; on the floor — anywhere....

KING.

Here?

ANNE.

Yes, yes! maleine *moves slightly.* KING. Oh!

ANNE.

What? What?

KING. r*Imitating* Maleine's *movement.* She has!... ANNE.

She is dead; she is dead. Come here.

KING.

I?

ANNE.

Yes. Her nose is bleeding. — Give me your handkerchief.

KING.

My... my handkerchief?

ANNE.

Yes.

KING.

No, no! not mine! not mine!

Here the Madman appears at the window, which has remained open, and suddenly chuckles.

ANNE.

There is somebody there! There is somebody at the window.

KING.

Oh! Oh! Oh!

ANNE.

It is the Madman! He has seen the light. — He will tell all. —Kill him!

The King runs to window and strikes the

Madman with his sword.

THE MADMAN.

Falling. Oh! Oh! Oh! ANNE.

Is he dead?

KING.

He has fallen! He has fallen into the

moat. He is drowning! Hark! Hark!...

Sounds of water-splash audible. ANNE.

Is there any one in the neighborhood?

KING.

He is drowning; he is drowning! Listen!

ANNE.

Is there any one in the neighborhood?

Thunder and lightning. KING.

Lightning! Lightning!

ANNE.

What?

KING.

It rains! it rains! it hails! it hails! It thunders! it thunders!

ANNE.

What are you doing there at the window?

KING.

It is raining! It is raining on me! — it is pouring on my head! I wish I were on the lawn! I wish I were out of doors! it is pouring on my head! It would take all the water of the Flood to baptize me, now! The whole sky is shattering hail on my head! The whole sky is shattering lightnings on my head!

ANNE.

You are going mad! You will get struck by lightning!

KING.

It is hailing; it is hailing upon my head. The hailstones are like crows' eggs.

ANNE.

You are going mad! You will get stoned to death. — You are bleeding already. — Close the window.

KING.

I am thirsty.

ANNE.

Drink, then. There is some water in this glass.

KING.

Where?

ANNE.

There; it is still half full.

KING.

Did she drink from this glass?

ANNE.

Yes; perhaps.

KING.

Is there no other glass?

Empties the glass and rinses it. ANNE.

No, — what are you doing?

KING.

She is dead. *Strange sounds of rubbing*

and a noise of paws against the door. Oh!

ANNE.

There is a scratching at the door!

KING.

They scratch! they scratch!

ANNE.

Be quiet!

KING.

It is not a hand.

ANNE.

I do not know what it is.

KING.

Let us take care! Oh! Oh! Oh I ANNE.

Hjalmar! Hjalmar! What is the matter with you?

KING.

What? What?

ANNE.

You frighten me! You are going to fall! Drink, — drink a little.

KING.

Yes, yes.

ANNE.

Some one is walking in the corridor.

KING.

He will come in.

ANNE.

Who will?

KING.

He — he — who — *Makes a gesture of scratching.* ANNE.

Be quiet. — Some one is singing.

VOICES.

In the corridor. *De profundis clamavi ad te, Domine: Do mine, exaudi vocem meam /* ANNE.

It is the seven nuns going to the kitchen.

VOICES.

In the corridor. *Fiant aures tuce intendentes, in vocem deprecationis mea.* king lets fall the glass and decanter.

ANNE.

What have you done?

KING.

It is not my fault....

ANNE.

They must have heard the noise.... They will come in....

VOICES.

Retreating down the corridor.-Si' iniquitates observaveris, Domine: Domine, quis sustinebit? ANNE.

They have gone; they are going to the

kitchen.

KING.

Let me go too! Let me go too! Let me go with them! Open the door for me! *Goes to the door.* ANNE. *Holding him back.* What are you about? Where are you going? Are you mad? KING.

I wish to go with them! They are already on the lawn.... They are at the edge of the pool now.... There is a breeze; it is raining; there is water; there is air! — Oh! if you had at least put her to death in the open air! But here, in a little room! — In a poor little room! I am going to open the windows.

ANNE.

But it thunders! Are you going mad? I would have done better to come alone...
.

KING.

Yes! yes!

ANNE.

You would have washed your hands of it, would you not? But now...

KING.

I did not kill her! I had no hand in it. It was you who killed her. 'T was you j 't was you j 't was you!

ANNE.

Well; well; be quiet. — We will see afterwards. Only do not scream so.

KING.

Do not say it was I again, or I will kill you too. 'T was you! 'T was you!

ANNE.

Oh, do not shout like one possessed! They will hear you at the other end of the corridor.

KING.

Have I been heard? *Knocking at the door.* ANNE.

   Some one is knocking. Do not stir. *Knocking.* KING.

What is going to happen? What is going to happen now? *Knocking.* ANNE.

   Put out the light.

KING.

Oh!

ANNE.

I tell you to put out the light.

KING.

No, ANNE.

   I will put it out myself.
Puts the light out. Knocking.
Nurse *without).* Maleine! Maleine!

ANNE.

It is the nurse KING.

   Oh! oh! The nurse, the good, good nurse! Let me see the nurse! Let us open the door! Let us open the door!

ANNE.

Be silent; for God's sake, be silent.

   Nurse *(without).* Maleine! Maleine! Are you asleep?

KING.

Yes; yes; yes; oh!

ANNE.

Be silent!

   Nurse *(without.)*

   Maleine! — my poor little Maleine! — You no longer answer? You no longer wish to answer me? — She must be in a deep sleep.

KING.

Oh! Oh! — a deep sleep! *Knocking.*

ANNE.

   Be silent!

   Nurse *(without).*

   Maleine!— my poor little Maleine! I have brought you some beautiful white grapes and a little broth. They say you cannot eat; but I know you are very weak; I know you are hungry. — Maleine! Maleine! Let me in.

KING.

Oh! Oh! Oh!

ANNE.

Do not weep. She will go...

   Nurse *without).*

   Good heavens! here comes Hjalmar with little Allan. He will see that I have brought her some fruit. Let me hide it under my cloak.

   King.

   Hjalmar is coming!

ANNE.

Yes.

KING,

And little Allan.

ANNE.

I know it. Be silent!

HJALMAR *(without).*

Who's there?

   Nurse *(without).* Lt is I, my lord.

HJALMAR *(without).*

Oh! it is you, nurse. It is so dark in this corridor... I did not recognize you. What are you doing here?

   Nurse *(without).*

   I was on my way to the kitchen; and I

saw the dog in front of the door....

HJALMAR *(without).*

Oh! it's Pluto!— Here, Pluto!

ANNE.

It was the dog.

KING.

What?

ANNE.

It was the dog that was scratching —

   Nurse *(without).*

   He was in Maleine's room. I cannot tell Ijow he got out.„„ HJALMAR *without).*

   Is she no longer in her room?

   Nurse *(without).* I do not know; she does not answer.

HJALMAR *(without).*

She is asleep.

   Nurse *(without).* He will not get away from the door.

HJALMAR *(without)*

Leave him alone; dogs have strange notions. But what a storm, nurse! What a storm!...

   Nurse *(without).* And little Allan not abed yet!

   Hjalmar *(without).*

   He is looking for his mother; he cannot find his mother.

LITTLE ALLAN *(without).*

My ma-a-ma is lost.

HJALMAR *(without).*

He insists upon seeing her before going to sleep. He has not had her blessing. You do not know where she is,

   Nurse *without).*

   No.

LITTLE ALLAN *(without).*

My raa-a-ma is lost.

   Hjalmar *(without).* She cannot be found.

LITTLE ALLAN *(without).*

My raa-a-ma is lost, lo-ost, lo-ost. Oh! Oh! Oh!

KING.

Oh!

ANNE.

He is sobbing.

   Nurse *without).*

   Come, do not weep; here is your ball; I found it in the garden.

LITTLE ALLAN *(without).*

Oh! Oh! Oh!

   Muffled strokes against the door.

KING.

Listen! listen!

ANNE.

It is little Allan playing ball against the doorKING.

They will come in. — I am going to lock the door.

ANNE.

It is locked.

KING. *Going to the door.* The bolts! the bolts! ANNE.

Gently! Gently!

HJALMAR *without).*

Why is the dog sniffing under the door so?

Nurse *without).*

He wants to be let in; he is always with Maleine.

Hjalmar *without).*

Do you think she will be able to go out to-morrow?

Nurse *without).*

Yes, yes. She is cured. — Well, Allan, what are you doing there? — You have quit play? You listen at doors? Oh, the naughty little boy, listening at doors!

LITTLE ALLAN *without).*

There is a little bo-oy behind the door!

ANNE.

What does he say?

HJALMAR (*without).*

You should never listen at doors. Misfortunes come from listening at doors.

LITTLE ALLAN *(Without).*

There is a little bo-oy behind the door!

ANNE.

He has heard you!...

KING.

Yes; yes; I think he has.

ANNE.

He hears your heart or your teeth.

KING.

Can my teeth be heard?

ANNE.

I hear them even here. Close your mouth tightly.

KING.

I?

ANNE.

Now, do not lie down against the door. Go away.

KING.

Where? where?

ANNE.

Here! here!

LITTLE ALLAN *(withouf).*

There is a little bo-oy behind the door.

HJALMAR *(Without).*

Come away; you are sleepy.

Nurse *(without).* Come; you are a naughty little boy.

LITTLE ALLAN *(without).* 1 want to see the little bo-oy 1...

Nurse *(without).*

Yes; you shall see him to-morrow. Come, we are going now to find mamma. Do not cry. Come!

LITTLE ALLAN *without).*

I want to see the little boy. Oh! Oh! I will tell my ma-a-ma. Oh! Oh!

Nurse *without).*

And I shall tell mamma you waked Maleine. Come, Maleine is sick.

LITTLE ALLAN *without).*

Ma-a-leine is wo-orse?

Nurse *without).* Come; you will wake Maleine.

Little Allan *(without, more distant).*

No; no; I won't wake Ma-a-leine. I wo-on't wa-ke Ma-a-leine!

ANNE.

Have they gone?

KING.

Yes; yes. Let us go. I am going to open the door. The key! The key! Where is the key?

ANNE.

Here. — Wait a moment. — Let us carry her to her bed.

KING.

Who?

ANNE.

She...

KING.

I '11 have no more to do with it!

ANNE.

But they will see she was strangled. Help me!

KING.

I '11 have no more to do with it! Come I Come! Come!

ANNE.

Help me to take off the cord!

KING.

Come! Come!

ANNE.

I cannot take off the cord! A knife! A knife!

KING.

Oh! what has she about her neck? What is it that glitters about her neck? Come with me! Come with me!

ANNE.

It is nothing. It is a necklace of rubies. Your knife!

KING.

I '11 have no more to do with it! I '11 have no more to do with it, I tell you. Were the dear God on his knees before me!... I would sweep Him out of the way; I would sweep Him out of the way! I '11 have no more to do with it! Oh! here is — here is...

ANNE.

What? What?

KING.

Here is!... Oh! Oh! Oh!

Opens the door, feeling his way, and flees. ANNE.

Where is he?... He has fled.... What did he see?... I see nothing.... He has run against the walls of the corridor.... He has fallen at the end of the corridor.... I will not stay here alone. *Exit.* ACT FIFTH.

Scene I. — *A part of the graveyard before the castle. A great crowd. The storm continues.* AN OLD WOMAN.

The lightning has struck the windmill.

ANOTHER WOMAN.

I saw it fall.

A PEASANT.

Yes, yes. A blue ball! A blue ball!

ANOTHER PEASANT.

The windmill is on fire; its sails are on fire!

A CHILD.

It is turning. It is turning still!

ALL.

Oh!

AN OLD MAN.

Did you ever see a night like this?

A PEASANT.

That?

SERVANT.

Yes; she is ill.

A Vagabond *(entering).* There is a huge man-of-war in the harbor.

ALL.

A huge man-of-war?

VAGABOND.

A huge black vessel; and no sailors to be seen about it.

AN OLD MAN.

It is the Last Judgment.

The moon appears above the castle.
ALL.

The moon! The moon! The moon!

It is black: it is black! What is the matter

A PEASANT.

A THIRD WOMAN.

The dead will rise!

A PILGRIM

I think it is the judgment of the dead!

A WOMAN.

Do not tread on the graves.

ANOTHER WOMAN. *To the children.* Do not tread on the tombstones!

A PEASANT.

Rushing in. One of the arches of the bridge has fallen in. ALL.

Of the bridge? What bridge?

PEASANT.

The stone bridge of the castle. You can no longer get into the castle.

AN OLD MAN.

I have no desire to get into it.

ANOTHER OLD MAN.

I would not be there!...

AN OLD WOMAN.

Nor I!

ANOTHER PEASANT.

There is nobody there. *A pause.* SOME WOMEN.

It opens!

OTHER WOMEN.

Let us be gone! Let us be gone!

They flee, terrified. THE MEN.

What now? What now?

ALL THE WOMEN.

No one knows. *Exeunt, running.* SOME MEN.

Why, what can have happened?

OTHER MEN.

Nothing! nothing! *Exeunt, running.*

ALL.

But why are you running? There's nothing the matter! Nothing the matter!

Exeunt, running.

A CRIPPLE.

A window is opening.... A window is opening.... They are afraid.... There's nothing the matter!

Crawls off, terrified, on his hands.

HJALMAR.

What time is it?

FIRST LORD.

Nine o'clock.

HJALMAR.

We have been waiting for the King for more than an hour!

THIRD LORD.

No one knows yet where he is?

HJALMAR.

The seven nuns saw him last in the corridor.

SECOND LORD.

About what time?

HJALMAR.

About seven.

SECOND LORD.

Had he given no indication of...?

HJALMAR.'

He said nothing. Something must have happened. I am going to see. *Exit.* SECOND LORD.

One knows not what may happen on such nights.

THIRD LORD.

But Queen Anne, where is she?

FIRST LORD.

She was with him.

THIRD LORD.

Oh! well then!

SECOND LORD.

On such a night!

FIRST LORD.

Beware! The walls are listening....

Enter Chamberlain,

All.

Well?

CHAMBERLAIN.

No one knows where he is....

A LORD.

Some misfortune must have happened to him.

CHAMBERLAIN.

We must wait. I have been all over the castle. I have questioned everybody. No one knows where he is.

A LORD.

It must be time we were at chapel; listen, the seven nuns are there already.

_Distant chanting. ANOTHER LORD. *At window.* Come here! Come here! Look at the river. LORDS, *Running.* What is the matter?

A LORD.

There are three ships in the storm!

A MAID OF HONOR.

I dare not look at such a river any longer.

ANOTHER MAID OF HONOR.

Do not lift the curtains! Do not lift the curtains!

A LORD.

All the walls shake as though they had the fever.

ANOTHER LORD. *At another window.* Here, here; come here. SEVERAL.

What?

OTHERS.

I will not look out any more.

LORD.

All the animals have taken refuge in the graveyard! There are peacocks in the cypresses. There are owls on the tombstones. All the sheep of the village are crouching on the graves.

ALL.

What is it?

THE OLD LORD.

A dog howling.

A WOMAN.

Do not open that window again.

Enter Prince Hjalmar. 1 A Lord. Prince Hjalmar!

All.

You have seen him, my lord?

Hjalmar. I have seen nothing!

SEVERAL LORDS.

Why, then?...

HJALMAR.

I know nothing about it.

Enter Angus. ANGUS.

Open the doors! The King is coming.

ALL.

You have seen him?

ANGUS.

You will see!

A LORD.

Open the doors! I hear him.

ANNE. *Without.* Go in, sire. KING. *Without.* I am ill.... I shall not in.... I would rather not go to chapel.. ANNE. *At the door.* Go in! Go in! *Enter the* King *and* Queen Anne,

King.

I am ill.... Do not mind me....

HJALMAR.

You are ill, father?

King.

Yes, yes..

HJALMAR.

What ails you?

King.

I do not know.

ANNE.

It is this fearful night!

KING.
Ay, a fearful night!
ANNE.
Let us go to prayers.
KING.
But why are you all silent?
HJALMAR.
Father, what is that on your hair?
KING.
On my hair?
HJALMAR.
There is blood upon your hair.
KING.
Upon my hair? — Oh! it is my own. *Laughter.* — But why do you laugh? It is no laughing matter.
ANNE.
He had a fall in the corridor.
Knocking at the.little door.
A LORD.
Some one is knocking at the little door....
KING.
Ay, there is knocking at all the doors here! I will have no more knocking at the doors!
ANNE. *To a lord.* Sir, will you go see...?
LORD. *Opening the door.* It is the nurse, madam. KING.
Who?
LORD.
The nurse, sire.
ANNE. *Rising.* Wait, it is for me.... HJAL-MAR.
But let her come in! let her come in!
Enter Nurse.
NURSE.
I think it is raining into Maleine's room.
KING.
What?
NURSE.
I think it is raining into Maleine's room.
ANNE.
You must have heard the rain against the panes.
NURSE.
May I not open the door?
ANNE.
No! no! She needs rest.
NURSE.
May I not go in?
ANNE.
No; no; no!
KING.

No; no; no!
NURSE.
You would say the King had fallen in the snow.
KING.
What?
ANNE.
Now, what are you doing here? Begone! begone! *Exit* Nurse.
Hjalmar..
She is right. Your hair seems to be all white. Is it an effect of light?
ANNE.
Yes, there is too much light.
KING.
But why do you all look at me so? — Have you never seen me before?
ANNE.
Come; let us go into the chapel; the office will be finished. Come, come.
KING.
No, no, I would rather not pray to-night.
HJALMAR.
Not pray, father?
KING.
Yes, yes; but not in the chapel.... I do not feel well... not at all well.
ANNE.
Sit down awhile, my lord.
HJALMAR.
Father, what is the matter?
ANNE.
Cease, cease; question him no further; he was taken unawares by the storm; let him have time to collect himself a little. — Let us speak of something else.
HJALMAR.
Shall we not see Princess Uglyane to-night?
ANNE.
No, not to-night; she is still sick.
KING. *To* Hjalmar. I would like to be in your place. HJALMAR.
One would think we too were ill? It seems to me we all look green to-night.
KING.
What do you mean?
HJALMAR.
What, father?
KING.
What do you mean? You had better speak out frankly?
ANNE.
You did not understand. — You were absorbed. — I was saying that Uglyane

is still ailing, though she is better.
ANGUS.
And Princess Maleine, Hjalmar?
HJALMAR.
You will see her here before the end of.
..
Here the small door which the Nurse had left ajar begins to bang in the wind. The lights flicker KING.
Rising. Oh! ANNE.
Be seated! be seated! It is the door banging. Be seated; it is nothing.
HJALMAR.
Father, what is the matter to-night?
ANNE.
Do not persist; he is ill. *To a lord.* Would you go and close the door?
KING.
Oh, close well the doors! — But why do you walk on tiptoe so?
HJALMAR.
Is there a corpse in the hall?
KING.
What? What?
HJALMAR.
He looks as if he were walking round a bier.
KING.
Why do you speak only of fearsome things to-night?
HJALMAR.
But, father!...
ANNE.
Let us talk of something else. Is there not some more cheerful subject?
A MAID OF HONOR.
Let us speak a little of Princess Maleine....
KING. *Rising.* Can it be that? Can it be... ? ANNE.
Be seated; be seated!
KING.
But do not speak of Pr...
ANNE.
Why should we not speak of Princess Maleine? — It seems to me the lights burn badly to-night.
HJALMAR.
The wind has blown out several of them!
KING.
Light them all. Yes, light them all. *Lamps are relighted.* It is too light now! Do you see me?
HJALMAR.

But, father!...

KING.

But why do you all look at me?

ANNE.

Put out the lights. His eyes are very weak. *One of the* Lords *rises io leave the room,* KING.

Where are you going?

LORD.

Sire, I...

KING.

You must remain; you must remain here. I allow no one to leave the hall. You must remain about me.

ANNE.

Be seated; be seated. You cast a gloom over everybody.

KING.

Is any one touching the tapestries?

HJALMAR.

Why, no, father!

KING.

There is one piece that...

HJALMAR.

It is the wind.

KING.

Why has that tapestry been hung there?

HJALMAR.

Why, it has always been there; it is the "Slaughter of the Innocents," KING.

I don't want to see it there! I don't want to see it there! Take it away!

The tapestry is pulled aside, and another appears, depicting "The Last Judgment." KING.

This has been done purposely!

HJALMAR.

Pray you, father?

KING.

Oh, avow it. You have done it purposely, and I know right well what you mean.

A MAID OF HONOR.

What says the King?

ANNE.

Do not mind him; he has been terrified by this awful night!

HJALMAR.

Father! my poor father! what is it ails you?

A MAID OF HONOR.

Sire, will you have a glass of water?

KING.

Yes, yes. —Oh! no! no! — Indeed, all I do, all I do.., HJALMAR.

My father! Sire...

A MAID OF HONOR.

The King is distracted.

HJALMAR.

My father!...

ANNE.

Sire, your son speaks to you.

HJALMAR.

Father, why do you keep turning your head?

KING.

Wait a little! Wait a little!

HJALMAR.

But why do you turn your head?

KING.

I felt something on my neck..

ANNE.

Come, come, do not be afraid of everything.

HJALMAR.

There is no one behind you.

ANNE.

Say no more... say no more. Let us go into the chapel. Do you hear the nuns?

Muffled distant chanting. Queen Anne goes to the chapel door. The King follows her and then returns to his seat.

KING.

No; no! Do not open the doors yet!

ANNE.

Are you afraid to enter? — Why, there is no more danger there than here. Why should the lightning strike the chapel rather than elsewhere? Let us go in.

KING.

Let us wait a little longer. Let us stay here together. — Do you think God forgives everything? I have always loved you so far. — I have never done you harm — so far — so far, have I?

ANNE.

Come, come, no one questions that. — It seems the storm has caused great damage.

ANGUS.

They say the swans have flown away.

HJALMAR.

There is one that is dead.

KING. *Startled.* Well, well, say it, if you know it! You have made me suffer enough already! Out with it all, at once. But do not come here and... ANNE.

Be seated! be seated, pray!

HJALMAR.

Father! Father! What has happened?

KING.

Let us go in!

Lightning and thunder; one of the Seven Nuns throws the chapel door open outwards, and looks into the hall. The others are heard singing the litanies of the Blessed Virgin — "Rosa mystica, — ora pro nobis. — Turris davidica, etc., while a great red light from the stained-glass windows and the illumined tabernacle suddenly floods the King and Queen Anne.

KING.

Who arranged all this?

ALL.

What? What? What is the matter?

KING.

There is some one who knows all! There is some one here who has arranged all this; but *I* must know —

ANNE.

Tearing him away. Come away! Come away! KING.

There is some one who saw it!

ANNE.

Why, it is the moon.... Come away.

KING.

But it is damnable cowardice! There is some one who knows all! There is some one who saw it, and who dares not say so!

ANNE.

Why, it is the tabernacle!... Let us be gone!...

KING.

Yes! Yes! Yes!

ANNE.

Come away! Come away!

Exit hurriedly through the door opposite the chapel, with the King.

Several. Where are they going?

OTHERS.

What is the matter?

A LORD.

All the fir-woods are on fire!

ANGUS.

Misfortunes walk to-night. *Exeunt.*

Scene III. — *A corridor in the castle. The black dog scratching at a door. Enter* Nurse, *bearing a light.* NURSE.

That dog is still at Maleine's door! — Pluto! Pluto! What are you doing there? — Whatever can he mean by scratching at that door? — You will wake my poor Maleine! Away! Away! Away! *Stamps*

her foot. Good heavens, how scared he looks! Can it be that some accident has happened? Has any one trod on your paw, my poor Pluto! Come here, let us go to the kitchen! *Dog returns to the door.* Again at that door! Again at that door! But what is the matter, then, behind that door? Do you want to be near Maleine? — She is asleep; I hear nothing! Come! Come! You will wake her. *Enter* Prince Hjalmar. HJALMAR.
Who goes there?
NURSE.
It is I, my lord.
HJALMAR.
Oh! it is you, nurse? Here still?
NURSE.
I was going to the kitchen, and I noticed the black dog scratching at that door.
HJALMAR.
At that door again? Here, Pluto! Here Pluto!
NURSE.
Is the office finished?
HJALMAR.
Yes... my father was very strange to-night.
NURSE.
And the Queen in a bad humor!...
HJALMAR.
I believe he has the fever; we must watch over him. Great evils might come to pass....
NURSE.
Indeed, evils are not asleep.
HJALMAR.
I do not know what is happening to-night! It is not well — what is happening to-night. He is scratching at that door again!...
NURSE.
Here, Pluto! Give me your paw!
HJALMAR.
I am going to the garden for awhile.
NURSE.
Has it stopped raining?
HJALMAR.
I think not.
NURSE.
He is scratching at that door again! Here, Pluto! Come here! Sit up, Pluto, sit up!
    The dog barks.
HJALMAR.
Don't bark now.... I will lead him away.

He will end by waking Maleine. Come, Pluto! Pluto! Pluto!
NURSE.
He is back again at the door.
HJALMAR.
He will not leave that door?
NURSE.
But what is there, then, behind the door?
HJALMAR.
He must go away. Go away! Go away! *Kicks the dog, who howls, but returns scratch at the door.*
NURSE.
He is scratching, scratching and sniffing.
HJALMAR.
He smells something under the door.
NURSE.
There must be something....
HJALMAR.
Go and look....
NURSE.
The room is locked; I have not the key.
HJALMAR.
Who has the key?
NURSE.
Queen Anne.
HJALMAR.
Why does she have the key?
NURSE.
I know nothing about it.
HJALMAR.
Knock gently.
NURSE.
I shall wake her.
HJALMAR.
Let us listen!
NURSE.
I hear nothing.
HJALMAR.
Knock softly. *She knocks gently three times.* NURSE.
    I hear nothing.
HJALMAR.
Knock a little louder.
    As she knocks the last time, the tocsin sounds suddenly as though it were being rung within the chamber.
NURSE.
Ah!
HJALMAR.
The bells! The tocsin!
NURSE.
The window must be open.
HJALMAR.

Yes, yes, go in!
NURSE.
The door is open!
HJALMAR.
Was it locked?
NURSE.
It was locked just now!
HJALMAR.
Go in! nurse *enters the chamber.*
    Nurse. *Coming out of the chamber.* My light was blown out as I opened the door.... But I saw something....
HJALMAR.
What? What?
NURSE.
I do not know. The window is open. — I think she has fallen...
HJALMAR.
Maleine?
NURSE.
Yes. — Quick! quick!
HJALMAR.
What?
NURSE.
A light!
HJALMAR.
I have none.
NURSE.
There is a lamp at the end of the corridor. Go fetch it!
HJALMAR.
I will. *Exit.* NURSE.
In the doorway.' Maleine! Where are you, Maleine? Maleine! Maleine! Maleine! *Re-enter* Hjalmar. HJALMAR.
I cannot unfasten it. Where is your lamp? I will go light it from the other. *Exit.* NURSE.
    Yes. — Maleine! Maleine! Maleine! Are you ill? It is I! My God! My God! Maleine! Maleine! Maleine!
Re-enter Hjalmar *with the light.* HJAL-MAR.
Go in!
Hands light to Nurse, *who re-enters the room.* Nurse. *From within the room.* Ah! HJALMAR. *In the doorway.* What now? What now? What is the matter?
NURSE.
She is dead! I tell you, she is dead! She is dead! she is dead!
HJALMAR.
She is dead? Maleine dead!
NURSE.
Yes! yes! yes! yes! yes! Come in! come

in! come in!

HJALMAR. *Entering chamber.* Dead? Is she dead? NURSE.

Maleine! Maleine! Maleine She is cold 1 I believe she is cold!

HJALMAR.

She is cold.

NURSE.

Oh! Oh! Oh! *Wind bangs and closes the door.*

Scene IV. — Princess Maleine's *chamber.*

Hjalmar *and* Nurse. *During the whole of this scene the tocsin is heard sounding without.*

Nurse. Help me! Help me!

HJALMAR.

What? How? How?

NURSE.

She is stiff. My God! My God! Maleine! Maleine!

HJALMAR.

But her eyes are open!....

NURSE.

She has been strangled! Her neck, her neck, her neck! See!

HJALMAR.

Yes! yes! yes!

NURSE.

Call! Call! Shout!

HJALMAR.

Yes, yes, yes. Oh! Oh! — *Exit. Without.* Hurry! hurry! Strangled! Strangled! Maleine! Maleine! Maleine! Strangled! Strangled! Strangled! Oh! Oh! Oh r Strangled! Strangled! Strangled!

He is heard rushing down the corridor, beat ing the doors and the walls.

A MAN-SERVANT.

7» the corridor." What's happened? What's happened? What's happened? HJALMAR. *In the corridor.* Strangled! Strangled! NURSE.

Maleine! Maleine! Help! Help!

MAN-SERVANT. *Entering.* It was the madman! He has been found under the window! NURSE.

The madman!

MAN-SERVANT.

Yes! yes! He is in the moat! He is dead! NURSE.

The window is open!

MAN-SERVANT.

Oh! poor little Princess!

Enter Angus, Lords, Ladies, Maids, Servants, *and the* Seven Nuns, *with lights.* ALL.

What is it? — What has happened?

Man-servant. Some one has killed the little Princess....

Several.

Some one has killed the little Princess?...

OTHERS.

Maleine?

MAN-SERVANT.

Yes, I think it was the madman.

A LORD.

I told you misfortunes were coming!

NURSE.

Maleine! Maleine! My poor little Maleine!... Help me.

A NUN.

There's nothing to be done!

ANOTHER NUN.

She is cold!

THIRD NUN.

She is rigid!

FOURTH NUN.

Close her eyes.

FIFTH NUN.

They are set.

SIXTH NUN.

Her hands must be folded.

SEVENTH NUN.

It is too late.

A LADY.

Fainting. Oh! Oh! Oh! NURSE.

Help me to lift Maleine! Help me! My God! My God! Help me!

MAN-SERVANT.

She weighs no more than a bird.

A great outcry in the corridor KING. *Without.* Ah! Ah! Ah! Ah! All! They have seen it! They have seen it! I am coming! I'm coming! I'm coming! ANNE. *Without.* Stop! Stop! You are mad! KING.

Come along! Come along! With me! With me! *Enter* King, *dragging* Queen Anne *along.* She and I! I wouid rather out with it, at last. We did it, between us!

ANNE.

He has gone mad! Help me.

KING.

No, I am not mad. She killed Maleine!

ANNE.

He is mad. Take him away! He is hurting me! Some dreadful thing will happen.

KING.

It was she! It was she! And I! I! I! I was here, too.

HJALMAR.

What? What?

KING.

She strangled her. So! So! Look! look! look! Some one was knocking at the windows! Ah! ah! ah! ah! ah! I see her red cloak there, over Maleine! Look! look! look!

HJALMAR. *To* Queen Anne. How came that red cloak here? ANNE.

But what has happened?

HJALMAR.

How came that cloak here?

ANNE.

But you can see he is mad.

HJALMAR.

Answer me I how came it here?

ANNE.

Is it mine?

HJALMAR.

Ay, yours! yours! yours! yours 1 ANNE.

Oh, let me go! You hurt me.

HJALMAR.

How came it here! how? how? — You have...

ANNE.

Well? Well?

HJALMAR.

Oh, you whore! whore! whore! raonstr — monstrous whore!.. There! There! There! There! There! *Stabs her repeatedly.* ANNE.

Oh! Oh! Oh! *She dies.* SEVERAL.

He has stabbed the Queen!

OTHERS.

Seize him!

HJALMAR.

You will poison the crows and the worms!

ALL.

She is dead!...

ANGUS.

Hjalmar! Hjalmar!

HJALMAR.

Leave me, leave me! — So! So! So! *Stabbing himself.'* Maleine! Maleine! Maleine! — Oh, father! father!... *Falls.*

KING.

Oh! Oh! oh!

HJALMAR.

Maleine! Maleine! Give me her little

hand. — Oh! Oh! Open the windows! Yes, yes! Oh! Oh! *He dies.* NURSE.

A handkerchief! A handkerchief! He will die!

ANGUS.

He is dead.

NURSE.

Raise him. The blood is choking him.

A LORD.

He is dead.

KING.

Oh! Oh! Oh! I had never wept since the Flood. But now I am in hell up to the eyes. — Oh! look, look, at their eyes. They will leap out upon me like frogs!

ANGUS.

He is mad.

KING.

No, no, but I have lost all courage!... Oh, it is enough to draw tears from the pavements of hell!

ANGUS.

Take him away; he can no longer bear the, sight of it.

KING.

No, no. Let me remain. I dare not be left alone any more. Where now is the fair Queen Anne? Anne!... Anne!... She is all distorted... I do not love her at all any more.... My God! How miserable one looks when dead! I would not kiss her any more now.... Put something over her....

NURSE.

And over Maleine, too.... Maleine! Maleine!... Oh! Oh! Oh!

KING.

I shall never kiss anybody again, in all my life, since I have seen all this. Where now is our poor little Maleine? *Takes* Maleine's */ia/ii/.J* — Oh! She is cold as an earth-worm. — She came down like an angel into my arms.... But 't was the wind that killed her!

ANGUS.

Let us take him away; for God's sake, let us take him away.

NURSE.

Yes! yes!

A LORD.

Let us wait a moment.

KING.

Have you any black feathers? We should have black feathers to know if the Queen still lives.... She was a beau-

tiful woman, do you know? — Do you hear my teeth?

The dawn comes into the room.

ALL.

What?

KING.

Do you hear my teeth?

NURSE.

It is the bells, my lord....

KING.

No; it is my heart, then! Oh! I loved them dearly, all three, you see! I should like to drink a little.

NURSE. *Bringing a glass of water.* Here is some water! KING.

Thank you. *_Drinks eagerly.* NURSE.

Do not drink so.... You are in a sweat.

KING.

I am so thirsty.

NURSE.

Come away, my poor lord! Let me wipe your forehead.

KING.

Yes! — Ale! You have hurt me. I fell in the corridor.... I was frightened.

NURSE.

Come away, come away. Let us go.

KING.

They will feel cold on the flag-stones!... She cried out; "Mamma!" and then, "Oh! Oh! Oh!" 'Tis pity, is it not? A poor little maid! But 't was the wind! Oh! never throw the windows open! It must have been the wind.... There were blind vultures in the wind to-night! — Do not let her little hands hang loose upon the floor. You are nearly treading on her hands. — Oh! Oh! Take care!

NURSE.

Come away; come away. Let every one go to bed. It is time. Come, come, KING.

Yes, yes, yes, it is too hot here.... Put out the lights, and let us go into the garden; it will be cool on the lawn after the rain. I want a little rest. Oh! look, the sun!

The sunlight enters the room NURSE.

THE GRANDFATHER.

Come away; come away; let us go into the garden.

KING.

But you must lock up little Allan! I will not have him come and frighten ine again!

NURSE.

Yes, yes, we shall lock him up. Come away; come away.

KING.

Have you the key?

NURSE.

Yes; come.

KING.

Yes; help me. I find it a little hard to walk.... I am a poor little old man. My legs no longer work; but my head is all right. *Leaning on the* Nurse. Am I not hurting you?

NURSE.

No, no; lean firmly.

KING.

You must not be angry with me, must you? I who am the oldest, I find it hard to die. There, there! now it's over. I am glad it is over; for I had the whole world on my heart.

NURSE.

Come away, my poor lord.

KING.

My God! My God! She is waiting now on the wharves of hell.

NURSE.

Come away! Come away!

KING.

Is there any one here that fears the curse of the dead?

ANGUS.

Ay, my lord, I do.

KING.

Well! close their eyes, then, and let us be gone.

NURSE.

Yes, yes. Come hence! Come hence!

KING.

I come; I come. Oh! Oh! how lone 1 shall be now! I stand in woe up to my ears. At seventy-seven years! Where are you now?

NURSE.

Here! Here!

KING.

You will not be angry with me? — Let us go to breakfast. Will there be salad for breakfast? I should like a little salad. ...

NURSE.

Yes; yes. There will be some.

KING.

I do not know why; I am a little sad to-day. — My God! My God! How unhappy the dead look! *Exit with* Nurse. AN-

GUS.

Another night like this, and all our heads will be white.

Exeunt all, except the Seven Nuns, who intone the *Miserere,* while carrying the corpses to _ the bed. The bells cease. Nightingales 'are heard without. A cock jumps on the window-sill and crows. Persons.

The Grandfather. *(He is Hind.)*
The Father.
The Uncle.
The Three Daughters.
The Sister Of Charity.-
The Maid-servant.
The jcene in modern times.
The Intruder.

A gloomy room in an old chateau. A door on the right, a door on the left, and a small secret door in one corner. At the back, stained-glass windows, in which green is the dominant color, and a glass door opening upon a terrace. A big Dutch clock in a corner. A lighted lamp.

THE THREE DAUGHTERS.

Come here, grandfather. Sit under the lamp.

THE GRANDFATHER.

It seems to me it is not very light here.

THE FATHER.

Shall we go out on the terrace, or shall we stay in the room?

THE UNCLE.

Would n't it be better to stay here? It has rained all the week, and the nights are damp and cold.

THE ELDEST DAUGHTER.

The stars are out, though.

THE UNCLE.

Oh, the stars — that makes no difference.

THE GRANDFATHER.

We had better stay here. You don't know what may happen.

THE FATHER.

We need h.ive no more anxiety. She is out of danger.. ,,.

THE GRANDFATHER.

I believe she is not doing well.

THE FATHER.

Why do you say that?

THE GRANDFATHER.

I have heard her voice.

THE FATHER.

But since the doctors assure us that we may be easy....

THE UNCLE.

You know quite well your father-in-law likes to alarm us needlessly.

THE GRANDFATHER.

I dp not see things as y u dp.

THE UNCLE.

Then you should trust to us, who do see. She was looking very well this afternoon. She is sleeping quietly now; and we are not going needlessly to poison the first pleasant evening fortune gives us.... It seems to me we have a right to rest, and even to laugh a little, without being afraid, this evening.

THE FATHER.

That is true; this is the first time I have felt at home, as if I were in my own household, since this terrible childbirth.

THE UNCLE.

Once sickness enters a house, it is as if there were a stranger in the family.

THE FATHER.

And then, you see, too, outside the family, you can count on no one.

THE UNCLE.

You are quite right.

THE GRANDFATHER.

Why couldn't I see my poor daughter to-day?

THE UNCLE.

You know very well that the doctor forbade it

I do not know what to think.

THE UNCLE.

It is useless to alarm yourself.

THE GRANDFATHER. *Pointing to the door on the left.* She cannot hear us?

THE FATHER.

We will not speak loudly enough; besides, the door is very thick, and then the Sister of Charity is with her, and will warn us if we are making too much noise.

THE GRANDFATHER. *Pointing to the door on the right.* He cannot hear us?

THE FATHER.

No, no.

THE GRANDFATHER.

He sleeps?

THE FATHER.

I suppose so.

THE GRANDFATHER.

We ought to go and see.

THE UNCLE.

He would give me more anxiety than your wife, this little fellow. It is several weeks since he was born, and he has hardly moved; he has not uttered a single cry yet; you would say he was a wax baby.

THE GRANDFATHER.

I believe he will be deaf, and perhaps dumb.... That is what comes of marrying cousins.... *Reproachful silence.* THE FATHER.

I am almost angry with him for the suffering he has caused his mother.

THE UNCLE.

You must be reasonable; it is not the poor little fellow's fault. — He is all alone in that room?

THE FATHER.

Yes; the doctor no longer allows him to remain in his mother's room.

THE UNCLE.

But the nurse is with him?

THE FATHER.

No; she has gone to rest a moment; she has well earned it these last few days. — Ursula, just run and see if he is asleep.

THE ELDEST DAUGHTER.

Yes, father.

The three sisters get up, and go into the room on the right, hand in hand THE FATHER.

At what time is our sister coming?

THE UNCLE.

About nine o'clock, I believe.

THE FATHER.

It is after nine. I would have liked her to come this evening; my wife was quite bent on seeing her.

THE UNCLE.

She is sure to come. Is it the first time she has ever come here?

THE FATHER.

She has never entered the house.

THE UNCLE.

It is very difficult for her to leave her convent.

THE FATHER.

She will be alone?

THE UNCLE.

I think one of the nuns will accompany her. They cannot go out alone, THE FATHER.

She is the Superior, though.

THE UNCLE.
The rule is the same for all.

THE GRANDFATHER.
You are no longer anxious?

THE UNCLE.
Why should we be anxious? There is no need to keep returning to that? There is nothing more to fear.

THE GRANDFATHER.
Your sister is older than you?

THE UNCLE.
She is the eldest of us all.

'THE GRANDFATHER.
I do not know what ails me; I feel uneasy. I wish your sister were here.

THE UNCLE.
She will come; she promised to.

THE GRANDFATHER.
I wish this evening were over!

The Three Daughters come in again

THE FATHER.
He sleeps?

THE ELDEST DAUGHTER.
Yes, father; very soundly.

THE UNCLE.
What shall we do while we are waiting?

THE GRANDFATHER.
Waiting for what?

THE UNCLE.
Waiting for our sister.

THE FATHER.
You see nothing coming, Ursula?

THE ELDEST DAUGHTER. _At the window._ No, father. THE FATHER.
And in the avenue? — You see the avenue?

THE DAUGHTER.
Yes, father; it is moonlight, and I see the avenue as far as the cypress wood.

THE GRANDFATHER.
And you see no one, Ursula?

THE DAUGHTER.
No one, grandfather.

THE UNCLE.
How is the weather?

THE DAUGHTER.
Very fine. Do you hear the nightingales?

THE UNCLE.
Yes, yes!

THE DAUGHTER.
A little wind is rising in the avenue.

THE GRANDFATHER.
A little wind in the avenue, Ursula?

THE DAUGHTER.

Yes; the trees are stirring a little.

THE UNCLE.
It is surprising that my sister should not be here yet.

THE GRANDFATHER.
I do not hear the nightingales any longer, Ursula.

THE DAUGHTER.
I believe some one has come into the garden, grandfather.

THE GRANDFATHER.
Who is it?

THE DAUGHTER.
I do not know; I see no one.

THE UNCLE.
Because there is no one there.

THE DAUGHTER.
There must be some one in the garden; the nightingales are silent all at once.

THE GRANDFATHER.
I hear no footsteps, though.

THE DAUGHTER.
It musf be that some one is passing near the pond, for the swans are frightened.

ANOTHER DAUGHTER.
All the fish of the pond are rising suddenly.

THE FATHER.
You see no one?

THE DAUGHTER.
No one, father.

THE FATHER.
But yet the pond is in the moonlight....

THE DAUGHTER.
Yes; I can see that the swans are frightened. THE UNCLE.
I am sure it is my sister that frightens them. She must have come in by the little gate.

THE FATHER.
I cannot understand why the dogs do not bark.

THE DAUGHTER.
I see the watch dog in the back of his kennel. — The swans are crossing to the other bank!...

THE UNCLE.
They are afraid of my sister. I will go and see. /fr _calls._J Sister! sister! Is it you? — There is no one there.

THE DAUGHTER.
I am sure that some one has come into the garden. You will see.

THE UNCLE.
But she would answer me.

THE GRANDFATHER.
Are not the nightingales beginning to sing again, Ursula?

THE DAUGHTER.
I no longer hear a single one in all the fields. THE GRANDFATHER.
And yet there is no noise.

THE FATHER.
There is a stillness of death.

THE GRANDFATHER.
It must be some stranger that frightens them, for if it were one of the household, they would not be silent.

THE DAUGHTER.
There is one on the big weeping willow. — It has flown away!...

THE UNCLE.
Are you going to talk about nightingales all night?

THE GRANDFATHER.
Are all the windows open, Ursula?

THE DAUGHTER.
The glass door is open, grandfather.

THE GRANDFATHER.
It seems to me that the cold comes into the room.

THE DAUGHTER.
There is a little wind in the garden, grandfather, and the rose leaves are falling.

THE FATHER.
Well, shut the door, Ursula. It is late.

THE DAUGHTER.
Yes, father. — I cannot shut the door, father.

THE TWO OTHER DAUGHTERS.
We cannot shut the door.

THE GRANDFATHER.
Why, children, what is the matter with the door?

THE UNCLE.
You need not say that in such an extraordinary voice. I will go and help them.

THE ELDEST DAUGHTER.
We do not quite succeed in closing it.

THE UNCLE.
It is because of the damp. Let us all push together.... There must be something between the doors.

THE FATHER.
The carpenter will set it right to-morrow.

THE GRANDFATHER.
Is the carpenter coming to-morrow?

THE DAUGHTER.

Yes, grandfather; he is coming to work in theejlar THE GRANDFATHER.

He will make a noise in the house!...

THE DAUGHTER.

I will tell him to work quietly.

All at once the sound of the sharpening of a scythe is heard outside.

THE GRANDFATHER.

Startled. Oh! THE UNCLE.

Ursula, what is that?

THE DAUGHTER.

I don't quite know; I think it is the gardener. I cannot see very well; he is in the shadow of the house.

THE FATHER.

It is the gardener going to mow.

THE UNCLE. j

He mows by night?

THE FATHER.

Is not to-morrow Sunday? — Yes. — I noticed that the grass was very high about the house.

4 THE GRANDFATHER.

It seems to me his scythe makes as much noise — THE DAUGHTER.

He is mowing near the house.

THE GRANDFATHER.

Can you see him, Ursula?

THE DAUGHTER.

No, grandfather; he is in the dark.

THE GRANDFATHER.

It seems to me his scythe makes as much noise — THE DAUGHTER.

That is because you have a very sensitive ear, grandfather.

THE GRANDFATHER.

I am afraid he will wake my daughter.

THE UNCLE.

We hardly hear him.

THE GRANDFATHER.

I hear him as if he were mowing in the house.

THE UNCLE.

She will not hear it; there is no danger.

THE FATHER.

It seems to me the lamp is not burning well this evening.

THE UNCLE.

It wants filling.

THE FATHER.

I saw it filled this morning. It has burnt badly ever since the window was shut.

THE UNCLE.

I think the chimney is dim.

THE FATHER.

It will burn better soon.

THE DAUGHTER.

Grandfather is asleep. He has not slept before for three nights.

THE FATHER.

He has been very worried.

THE UNCLE.

He always worries too much. There are times when he will not listen to reason.

THE FATHER.

It is quite excusable at his age.

THE UNCLE.

God knows what we shall be like at his age!

THE FATHER.

He is nearly eighty years old.

THE UNCLE.

Well, then, he has a right to be strange.

THE FATHER.

Perhaps we shall be stranger than he is.

THE UNCLE.

One does not know what may happen, odd sometimes.

THE FATHER.

He is like all the blind.

THE UNCLE.

They reflect too much.

THE FATHER.

They have too much time to spare.

THE UNCLE.

They have nothing else to do.

THE FATHER.

And, besides, they have no amusements.

THE UNCLE.

That must be terrible.

THE FATHER.

It seems they get used to it.

THE UNCLE.

I cannot imagine that.

THE FATHER.

They are certainly to be pitied.

THE UNCLE.

Not to know where one is, not to know whence one has come, not to know whither one is going, no longer to distinguish midday from midnight, nor summer from winter.... And always that darkness, that darkness!... I would rather not live.... Is it absolutely incurable?

THE FATHER.

It appears so.

THE UNCLE.

But he is not absolutely blind?

THE FATHER.

He can distinguish a strong light.

THE UNCLE.

Let us take care of our poor eyes.

THE FATHER.

He often has strange ideas.

THE UNCLE.

There are times when he is not amusing.

THE FATHER.

He says absolutely everything he thinks.

THE UNCLE.

But formerly he was not like this?

THE FATHER.

No; formerly he was as rational as we are; he never said anything extraordinary. It is true, Ursula encourages him a little too much; she answers all his questions — THE UNCLE.

It would be better not to answer. It's a mistaken kindness to him. *Ten o'clock strikes.* THE GRANDFATHER.

Waking up. Am I facing the glass door?

THE DAUGHTER.

You have had a good sleep, grandfather?

THE GRANDFATHER.

Am I facing the glass door?

THE DAUGHTER.

Yes, grandfather.

THE GRANDFATHER.

There is no one at the glass door?

THE DAUGHTER.

No, grandfather; I see no one.

THE GRANDFATHER.

I thought some one was waiting. No one has come, Ursula?

THE DAUGHTER.

No one, grandfather.

THE GRANDFATHER. *To the* Uncle *and* Father. And your sister has not come?

THE UNCLE.

It is too late; she will not come now. It is not nice of her.

THE FATHER.

I begin to be anxious about her.

A noise, as of some one coming into the house THE UNCLE.

She is here! Did you hear?

THE FATHER.

Yes; some one has come in at the basement, THE UNCLE.

It must be our sister. I recognized her step.

THE GRANDFATHER.

I heard slow footsteps.

THE FATHER.
She came in very softly.

THE UNCLE.
She knows there is sickness....

THE GRANDFATHER.
I hear nothing more now.

THE UNCLE.
She will come up immediately; they will tell her we are here.

THE FATHER.
I am glad she has come.

THE UNCLE.
I was sure she would come this evening.

THE GRANDFATHER.
She is a long time coming up.

THE UNCLE.
However, it must be she.

THE FATHER.
We are not expecting any one else.

THE GRANDFATHER.
I hear no noise in the basement.

THE FATHER.
I will call the maid. We must know what to expect. *He pulls the be 11-1 ope.* THE GRANDFATHER.
I hear a noise on the stairs already.

THE FATHER.
It is the maid coming up.

THE GRANDFATHER.
It seems to me she is not alone.

THE FATHER.
It is because the maid makes so much noise....

THE GRANDFATHER.
It seems to me she is not alone.

THE FATHER.
She is getting terribly stout; I believe she is dropsical.

THE UNCLE.
It is time you got rid of her; you will have her on your hands.

THE GRANDFATHER.
I hear your sister's step!

THE FATHER.
I hear no one but the maid.

THE GRANDFATHER.
It is your sister! It is your sister!.

A knock at the secret door. THE UNCLE.
She is knocking at the door of the private stairway.

THE FATHER.
I will go open it myself, because that little door makes too much noise; it is only used when we want to come up without being seen. *He partly opens the little*

door; the MaidServant *remains outside in the opening.* Where are you?

THE MAID-SERVANT.
Here, sir.

THE GRANDFATHER.
Your sister is at the door.

THE UNCLE.
I see no one but the maid.

THE FATHER.
There is no one there but the maid. *To the* Maid-servant. Who was it who came into the house?

THE MAID-SERVANT.
Came into the house, sir?

THE FATHER.
Yes; some one came just now?

THE SERVANT.
No one came, sir.

THE GRANDFATHER.
Who is it sighs so?

THE UNCLE.
It is the maid; she is out of breath.

THE GRANDFATHER.
Is she crying?

THE UNCLE.
Why, no; why should she be crying?

THE FATHER. *To the* Maid-Servant. No one came in just now? THE MAID-SER-VANT.
No, sir.

THE FATHER.
But we heard the door open!

THE MAID-SERVANT.
It was I shutting the door, sir.

THE FATHER.
It was open?

THE MAID-SERVANT.
Yes, sir.

THE FATHER.
Why was it open, at this hour?

THE MAID-SERVANT.
I do not know, sir. / had shut it.

THE FATHER.
But then who was it opened it?

THE MAID-SERVANT.
I do not know, sir. Some one must have gone out after me, sir.

THE FATHER.
You must be careful. — Don't push the door; you know what a noise it makes!.

THE MAID-SERVANT.
But I am not touching the door, sir.

THE FATHER.
But you are. You push as if you were trying to get into the room.

THE MAID-SERVANT.
But I am three steps away from the door, sir.

THE FATHER.
Don't talk quite so loudly.

THE GRANDFATHER.
Are you putting out the light?

THE ELDEST DAUGHTER.
No, grandfather.

THE GRANDFATHER.
It seems to me it is dark all at once.

THE FATHER. *To the* Maid-servant. You may go down now; but do not make so much noise on the stairs. THE MAID-SERVANT.
I did not make any noise on the stairs, sir.

THE FATHER.
I tell you, you made a noise. Go down softly; you will wake your mistress.

THE MAID-SERVANT.
It was not 1 who made a noise, sir.

THE FATHER.
And if any one comes now, say that we are not at home.

THE UNCLE.
Yes; say that we are not at home.

THE GRANDFATHER. *Shuddering.* You must not say that! THE FATHER. ... Except to my sister and the doctor. THE UNCLE.
When will the doctor come?

THE FATHER.
He will not be able to come before midnight.

He shuts the door. A clock is heard striking eleven.

THE GRANDFATHER.
She has come in?

THE FATHER.
Who, pray?

THE GRANDFATHER.
The maid.

THE FATHER.
Why, no; she has gone downstairs.

THE GRANDFATHER.
I thought she was sitting at the table.

THE UNCLE.
The maid?

THE GRANDFATHER.
Yes.

THE UNCLE.
Well, that's all that was lacking.

THE GRANDFATHER.
No one has come into the room?

THE FATHER.

Why no; no one has come in.

THE GRANDFATHER.

And your sister is not here?

THE UNCLE.

Our sister has not come. Where have your thoughts wandered?

THE GRANDFATHER.

You want to deceive me.

THE UNCLE.

Deceive you?

THE GRANDFATHER.

Ursula, tell me the truth, for the love of God!

THE ELDEST DAUGHTER.

Grandfather! Grandfather! what is the matter with you?

THE GRANDFATHER.

Something has happened!...-I am sure my daughter is worse!...

THE UNCLE.

Are you dreaming?

THE GRANDFATHER.

You do not want to tell me!... I see plainly there is something!...

THE UNCLE.

In that case you see better than we.

THE GRANDFATHER.

Ursula, tell me the truth.

THE DAUGHTER.

But we are telling you the truth, grandfather!

THE GRANDFATHER.

You are not speaking in your natural voice.

THE FATHER.

That is because you frighten her.

THE GRANDFATHER.

Your voice is changed, — yours, too!

THE FATHER.

But you are going mad!

He and the Uncle make signs to each other that the Grandfather has lost his reason.

THE GRANDFATHER.

I hear plainly that you are afraid.

THE FATHER.

But what should we be afraid of?

THE GRANDFATHER.

Why do you want to deceive me?

THE UNCLE.

Who thinks of deceiving you?

THE GRANDFATHER.

Why have you put out the light?

THE UNCLE.

But the light has not been put out; it is as light as before.

THE DAUGHTER.

It seems to me the lamp has gone down.

THE FATHER.

I see as well as usual.

THE GRANDFATHER.

I have millstones on my eyes! Children, tell me what is happening here! Tell me, for the love of God, you who can see! I am here, all alone, in darkness without end! I do not know who seats himself beside me! I do not know what is happening two steps from me!... Why were you speaking in a low voice just now?

THE FATHER.

No one spoke in a low voice.

THE GRANDFATHER.

You spoke in a low voice at the door.

THE FATHER.

You heard all I said.

THE GRANDFATHER.

You brought some one into the room.

THE FATHER.

But I tell you no one has come in!

THE GRANDFATHER.

Is it your sister or a priest? — You must not try to deceive me. — Ursula, who was it that came in?

THE DAUGHTER.

No one, grandfather.

THE GRANDFATHER.

You must not try to deceive me; I know what I know! — How many are we here?

THE DAUGHTER.

There are six of us about the table, grandfather.

THE GRANDFATHER.

You are all about the table?

THE DAUGHTER.

Yes, grandfather.

THE GRANDFATHER.

You are there, Paul?

THE FATHER.

Yes.

THE GRANDFATHER.

You are there, Oliver?

THE UNCLE.

Why, yes; why, yes; I am here, in my usual place. This is not serious, is it?

THE GRANDFATHER.

You are there, Genevieve?

ONE OF THE DAUGHTERS.

Yes, grandfather.

THE GRANDFATHER.

You are there, Gertrude?

ANOTHER DAUGHTER.

Yes, grandfather.

THE GRANDFATHER.

You are here, Ursula?

THE ELDEST DAUGHTER.

Yes, grandfather, by your side.

THE GRANDFATHER.

And who is that sitting there?

THE DAUGHTER.

Where do you mean, grandfather? is no one.

THE GRANDFATHER.

There, there — in the midst of us!

THE DAUGHTER.

But there is no one, grandfather.

THE FATHER.

We tell you there is no one!

THE GRANDFATHER.

But you do not see, any of you!

THE UNCLE.

Oh, come now; you are joking.

THE GRANDFATHER.

I have no wish to joke, I can assure you.

THE UNCLE.

Well, then, believe those that see.

THE GRANDFATHER. *Undecidedly.* I thought there was some one.... I believe I shall not live much longer.... THE UNCLE.

Why should we go to work to deceive you? What good would that do?

THE FATHER.

We ought clearly to tell you the truth.

THE UNCLE.

What good would it do to deceive each other?

THE FATHER.

You could not live long without finding it out.

THE GRANDFATHER.

I wish I were at home!

THE FATHER.

Put you are at home here THE UNCLE.

Are we not at home?

THE FATHER.

Are you among strangers?

THE UNCLE.

You are strange this evening.

THE GRANDFATHER.

It is you who seem strange to me!

THE FATHER.

Do you want anything?

THE GRANDFATHER.

I do not know what ails me.

THE UNCLE.

Will you take anything?

THE ELDEST DAUGHTER.

Grandfather! grandfather! What do want, grandfather?

THE GRANDFATHER.

Give me your little hands, my children.

THE THREE DAUGHTERS.

Yes, grandfather.

THE GRANDFATHER.

Why are you all three trembling, my children?

THE ELDEST DAUGHTER.

We are hardly trembling at all, grandfather.

THE GRANDFATHER.

I believe you are all three pale.

THE ELDEST DAUGHTER.

It is late, grandfather, and we are tired.

THE FATHER.

You must go to bed, and grandfather too would do better to take a little rest.

THE GRANDFATHER.

I could not sleep to-night!

THE UNCLE.

We will wait for the doctor.

THE GRANDFATHER.

Prepare me for the truth!

THE UNCLE.

But there is no truth!

THE GRANDFATHER.

Then I do not know what there is!

THE UNCLE.

I tell you there is nothing at all!

THE GRANDFATHER.

I would like to see my poor daughter!

THE FATHER.

But you know very well that is impossible; she must not be wakened needlessly.

THE UNCLE.

You will see her to-morrow.

THE GRANDFATHER.

We hear no sound in her room.

THE UNCLE.

I should be uneasy if I heard any sound.

THE GRANDFATHER.

It is very long since I saw my daughter... . I took her hands yesterday evening, but I could not see her!... I no longer know what she is becoming.... I no longer know how she is.... I am no longer familiar with her face.... She must have changed in these weeks!... I felt the little bones of her cheeks under my hands... . There is nothing but the darkness between her and me, and all of you!... This is not life — this is not living!... You sit there, all of you, with open eyes that look at my dead eyes, and not one of you has pity!... I do not know what ails me.... No one tells what ought to be told me.... And everything is terrifying when you dream of it!... But why do you not speak?

THE UNCLE.

What would you have us say, since you will not believe us?

THE GRANDFATHER.

You are afraid of betraying yourselves!

THE FATHER.

Do be reasonable now.

THE GRANDFATHER.

For a long time something has been hidden from me here!... Something has happened in the house.... But I begin to understand now I have been deceived too long! —

You think, then, that I shall never find out anything?— There are moments when I am less blind than you, you know!... Have I not heard you whispering, for days and days, as if you were in the house of some one who had hanged himself? — I dare not say what I know this evening.... But I will know the truth! I shall wait for you to tell me the truth; but I have known it for a long time, in spite of you!— And now, I feel that you are all as pale as the dead!

THE THREE DAUGHTERS.

Grandfather! grandfather! What is the matter, grandfather?

THE GRANDFATHER.

It is not of you that I speak, my children; no, it is not of you that I speak.... I know quite well you would tell me the truth, if they were not by!... And besides, I am sure they are deceiving you also.... You will see, children, you will see!... Do I not hear all three of you sobbing?

THE UNCLE.

For my part, I will not stay here.

THE FATHER.

Can my wife really be so ill?

THE GRANDFATHER.

You need not try to deceive me any longer it is too late now, and I know the truth better than you!...

THE UNCLE.

But after all we are not blind, are we?

THE FATHER.

Would you like to go into your daughter's room? There is a mistake here and a misunderstanding that should end. — Would you?... THE GRANDFATHER.

No, no; not now... not yet....

THE UNCLE.

You see plainly, you are not reasonable.

THE GRANDFATHER.

One never knows all that a man has been unable to say in his life!... Who was it made that noise?

THE ELDEST DAUGHTER.

It is the flickering of the lamp, grandfather.

THE GRANDFATHER.

It seems to me it is very unsteady — very unsteady.

THE DAUGHTER.

It is the cold wind that vexes it... it is the cold wind that vexes it....

THE UNCLE.

There is no cold wind, the windows are shut.

THE DAUGHTER.

I think it is going out.

THE FATHER.

The oil must be out.

THE DAUGHTER.

It has gone entirely out.

THE FATHER.

We cannot stay like this in the dark.

THE UNCLE.

Why not? I am already accustomed to it.

THE FATHER.

There is a light in my wife's room.

THE UNCLE.

We will take it by and by, when the doctor has come.

THE FATHER.

It is true, we see well enough; there is light from outside.

THE GRANDFATHER.

Is it light outside?

THE FATHER.

Lighter than here.

THE UNCLE.

For my part, I would as soon talk in the dark.

THE FATHER.

So would I. *Silence.* THE GRANDFATHER.

It seems to me the clock makes such

a noise!...

THE ELDEST DAUGHTER.

That is because we are not speaking now, grandfather.

THE GRANDFATHER.

But why are you all silent?

THE UNCLE.

Of what would you have us speak? — You are not in earnest to-night.

THE GRANDFATHER.

Is it very dark in the room?

THE UNCLE.

It is not very light. *Silence.* THE GRAND-FATHER.

I do not feel well, Ursula; open the window a little.

THE FATHER.

Yes, daughter; open the window a little; I begin to feel the want of air myself.

The girl opens the window.

THE UNCLE.

I positively believe we have stayed shut up too long.

THE GRANDFATHER.

Is the window open, Ursula?

THE DAUGHTER.

Yes, grandfather; it is wide open.

THE GRANDFATHER.

One would not have said it was open; there is not a sound outside.

THE DAUGHTER.

No, grandfather; there is not the least sound.

THE FATHER.

The silence is extraordinary!

THE DAUGHTER.

One could hear an angel's step.

THE UNCLE.

That is the reason I do not like the country.

THE GRANDFATHER.

I wish I could hear some sound. What time is it, Ursula?

THE DAUGHTER.

Almost midnight, grandfather.

Here the Uncle begins to walk up and down the room THE GRANDFATHER.

Who is it walking around like that?

THE UNCLE.

It is I! it is I! Do not be frightened! I feel the need of walking a little. *Silence.* — But I am going to sit down again, — I do not see where I am going. *Silence.*

THE GRANDFATHER.

I wish I were somewhere else!

THE DAUGHTER.

Where would you like to go, grandfather?

THE GRANDFATHER.

I do not know where, — into another room — no matter where! no matter where!...

THE FATHER.

Where should we go?

THE UNCLE.

It is too late to go anywhere else.

Silence. They are sitting motionless, round the table.

THE GRANDFATHER.

What is that I hear, Ursula?

THE DAUGHTER.

Nothing, grandfather; it is the leaves falling. Yes, it is the leaves falling on the terrace.

THE GRANDFATHER.

Go shut the window, Ursula.

THE DAUGHTER.

Yes, grandfather.

She shuts the window, comes back, and sits down.

THE GRANDFATHER.

I am cold. *Silence. The three sisters kiss each other.* What is it I hear now?

THE FATHER.

It is the three sisters kissing each other.

THE UNCLE.

It seems to me they are very pale this evening. *Silence.* THE GRANDFATHER.

What is it I hear now, Ursula?

THE DAUGHTER.

Nothing, grandfather; it is the clasping of my hands. *Silence.* THE GRANDFA-THER.

What is it I hear? what is it I hear, Ursula?

THE DAUGHTER.

I do not know, grandfather; perhaps my sisters — they are trembling a little.

THE GRANDFATHER.

I am afraid, too, my children.

Here a ray of moonlight penetrates through a corner of the stained glass, and spreads strange gleams here and there in the room. Midnight strikes, and at the last stroke it seems to some that a sound is heard, very vaguely, as of some one rising in all haste.

THE GRANDFATHER. *Shuddering with peculiar horror.* Who is it that rose? THE UNCLE.

No one rose!

THE FATHER.

I did not rise!

THE THREE DAUGHTERS.

Nor I!... Nor I!... Nor I!

THE GRANDFATHER.

Some one rose from the table!

THE UNCLE.

Light the lamp!

Here suddenly a wail of fright is heard ir the child's room, on the right; and thii wail continues, with gradations of terror until the end of the scene.

THE FATHER.

Listen! the child!

THE UNCLE.

He has never cried before!

THE FATHER.

Let us go and look!

THE UNCLE.

The light! The light!

At this moment a hurrying of head-long heavy steps is heard in the room on the left. — Then a deathly stillness. — They listen in a dumb terror, until the door opens slowly, and the light from the next room falls into that in which they are waiting. The Sister of Charity appears on the threshold, in the black garments of her order, and bows as she makes the sign of the cross, to announce the death of the wife. They understand, and, after a moment of hesitation and fright, silently enter the chamber of death, while the Uncle politely effaces himself at the doorstep, to let the three young girls pass. The blind man, left alone, rises and gropes excitedly about the table in the darkness.

THE GRANDFATHER.

Where are you going? — Where are you going? — My children! — They have left me all alone!

The Blind.

To Charles Van Lerberghe.

Persons.

The Priest.

Three Men Who Were Born Blind.

A Very Old Blind Man.

Fifth Blind Man *(who is also deaf).*

Sixth Blind Man *(who can distinguish light and darkness).*

Three Old Blind Women In Prayer.

A Very Old Blind Woman.

A Young Blind Girl.

A Blind Madwoman.

An Infant, *child of the* Madwoman.

A Dog.

The Blind.

An ancient Norland forest, with an eternal look, under a sky of deep stars.

In the centre, and in the deep of the night, a very old priest is sitting, wrapped in a great black cloak. The chest and the head, gently upturned and deathly motionless, rest against the trunk of a giant hollow oak. The face is fearsome pale and of an immovable waxen lividness, in which the purple lips fall slightly apart. The dumb, fixed eyes no longer look out from the visible side of Eternity and seem to bleed with immemorial sorrows and with tears. The hair, of a solemn whiteness, falls in stringy locks, stiff and few, over a face more illuminated and more weary than all that surrounds it in the watchful stillness of that melancholy wood. The hands, pitifully thin, are clasped rigidly over the thighs.

On the right, six old men, all blind, are sitting on stones, stumps and dead leaves.

On the left, separated from them by an uprooted tree and fragments of rock, six women, also blind, are sitting opposite the old men. Three among them pray and mourn without ceasing, in a muffled voice. Another is old in the extreme. The fifth, in an attitude of mute insanity, holds on her knees a little sleeping child. The sixth is strangely young, and her whole body is drenched with her beautiful hair. They, as well as the old men, are all clad in the same ample and sombre garments. Most of them are waiting, with their elbows on their knees and their faces in their hands; and all seem to have lost the habit of ineffectual gesture and no longer turn their heads at the stifled and uneasy noises of the Island. Tall funereal trees, — yews, weeping-willows, cypresses, — cover them with their faithful shadows. A cluster of long, sickly asphodels is in bloom, not far from the priest, in the night. It is unusually oppressive, despite the moonlight that here and there struggles to pierce for an instant the glooms of the foliage

First Blind Man *who was born blind).* He has n't come back yet?

Second Blind Man *(who also tvas born blind).* You have awakened me.

FIRST BLIND MAN.

I was sleeping, too.

Third Blind Man *(also born blind).* I was sleeping, too.

First Blind Man. He has n't come yet?

SECOND BLIND MAN.

I hear nothing coming.

THIRD BLIND MAN.

It is time to go back to the Asylum.

FIRST BLIND MAN.

We ought to find out where we are.

SECOND BLIND MAN.

It has grown cold since he left.

FIRST BLIND MAN.

We ought to find out where we are!

THE VERY OLD BLIND MAN,

Does any one know where we are?

THE VERY OLD BLIND WOMAN.

We were walking a very long while; we must be a long way from the Asylum.

FIRST BLIND MAN.

Oh! the women are opposite us?

THE VERY OLD BLIND WOMAN.

We are sitting opposite you.

FIRST BLIND MAN.

Wait, I am coming over where you are. *He rises and gropes in the dark.* — Where are you? — Speak! let me hear where you are!

THE VERY OLD BLIND WOMAN.

Here; we are sitting on stones.

FIRST BLIND MAN. *Advances and stumbles against the fallen tree and the rocks.* There is something between us.

SECOND BLIND. MAN.

We had better keep our places.

THIRD BLIND MAN.

Where are you sitting? — Will you come over by us?

THE VERY OLD BLIND WOMAN.

We dare not rise!

THIRD BLIND MAN.

Why did he separate us?

FIRST BLIND MAN.

I hear praying on the women's side.

SECOND-BLIND MAN.

Yes; the three old women are praying.

FIRST BLIND MAN.

This is no time for prayer!

SECOND BLIND MAN.

You will pray soon enough, in the dormitory!

The three old women continue their prayers.

THIRD BLIND MAN.

I should like to know who it is I am sitting by.

SECOND BLIND MAN.

I think I am next to you. *They feel about the?n.* THIRD BLIND MAN.

We can't reach each other.

FIRST BLIND MAN.

Nevertheless, we are not far apart. *He feels about him and strikes with his staff the fifth blind man, who utters a muffled groan.* The one who cannot hear is beside us.

SECOND BLIND MAN.

I don't hear everybody; we were six just now.

FIRST BLIND MAN.

I am going to count. Let us question the women, too; we must know what to depend upon. I hear the three old women praying all the time; are they together?

THE VERY OLD BLIND WOMAN.

They are sitting beside me, on a rock.

FIRST BLIND MAN.

I am sitting on dead leaves.

THIRD BLIND MAN.

And the beautiful blind girl, where is she?

IE VERY OLD BLIND WOMAN.

She is near them that pray.

SECOND BLIND MAN.

Where is the mad woman, and her child?

THE YOUNG BLIND GIRL.

He sleeps; do not awaken him!

FIRST BLIND MAN.

Oh! how far away you are from us! I thought you were opposite me!

THIRD BLIND MAN.

We know — nearly — all we need to know. Let us chat a little, while we wait for the priest to come back.

THE VERY OLD BLIND WOMAN.

He told us to wait for him in silence.

THIRD BLIND MAN.

We are not in a church.

THF VERY OLD BLIND WOMAN.

You do not know where we are.

THIRD BLIND MAN.

I am afraid when I am not speaking.

SECOND BLIND MAN.

Do you know where the priest went?

THIRD BLIND MAN.

I think he leaves us for too long a time.

FIRST BLIND MAN.

He is getting too old. It looks as though he himself has no longer seen for some time. He will not admit it, for fear another should come to take his place among us; but I suspect he hardly sees at all any more. We must have another guide; he no longer listens to us, and we are getting too numerous. He and the three nuns are the only people in the house who can see; and they are all older than we are! — I am sure he has misled us and that he is looking for the road. Where has he gone?

— He has no right to leave us here....

THE VERY OLD BLIND MAN.

He has gone a long way: I think he said so to the women.

FIRST BLIND MAN.

He no longer speaks except to the women?

— Do we no longer exist? — We shall have to complain of him in the end.

THE VERY OLD BLIND MAN.

To whom will you complain?

FIRST BLIND MAN.

I don't know yet; we shall see, we shall see. — But where has he gone, I say? — I am asking the women.

THE VERY OLD BLIND WOMAN.

He was weary with walking such a long time. I think he sat down a moment among us. He has been very sad and very feeble for several days. He is afraid since the physician died. He is alone. He hardly speaks any more. I don't know what has happened. He insisted on going out to-day. He said he wished to see the Island, a last time, in the sunshine, before winter came. The winter will be very long and cold, it seems, and the ice comes already from the North. He was very uneasy, too: they say the storms of the last few days have swollen the river and all the dikes are shaken. He said also that the sea frightened him; it is troubled without cause, it seems, and the coast of the Island is no longer high enough. He wished to see; but he did not tell us what he saw. — At present, I think he has gone to get some bread and water for the mad woman. He said he would have to go a long way, perhaps. We must wait.

THE YOUNG BLIND GIRL.

He took my hands when he left; and his hands shook as if he were afraid. Then he kissed me FIRST BLIND MAN.

Oh! oh!

THE YOUNG BLIND GIRL.

I asked him what had happened. He told me he did not know what was going to happen. He told me the reign of old men was going to end, perhaps....

FIRST BLIND MAN.

What did he mean by saying that?

THE YOUNG BLIND GIRL.

I did not understand him. He told me he was going over by the great lighthouse.

FIRST BLIND MAN.

Is there a lighthouse here?

THE YOUNG BLIND GIRL.

Yes, at the north of the Island. I believe we are not far from it. He said he saw the light of the beacon even here, through the leaves. He has never seemed more sorrowful than to-day, and I believe he has been weeping for several days. I do not know why, but I wept also without seeing him. I did not hear him go away. I did not question him any further. I was aware that he smiled very gravely; I was aware that he closed his eyes and wished to be silent....

FIRST BLIND MAN.

He said nothing to us of all that!

THE YOUNG BLIND GIRL.

You do not listen when he speaks!

THE VERY OLD BLIND WOMAN.

You all murmur when he speaks!

SECOND BLIND MAN.

He merely said "Good-night" to us when he went away.

THIRD BLIND MAN.

It must be very late.

FIRST BLIND MAN.

He said "Good-night" two or three times when he went away, as if he were going to sleep. I was aware that he was looking at me when he said "Good-night; good-night." — The voice has a different sound when you look at any one fixedly.

FIFTH BLIND MAN.

Pity the blind!

FIRST BLIND MAN.

Who is that, talking nonsense?

SECOND BLIND-MAN.

I think it is he who is deaf.

FIRST BLIND MAN.

Be quiet! — This is no time for begging!

THIRD BLIND MAN.

Where did he go to get his bread and water?

THE VERY OLD BLIND WOMAN.

He went toward the sea.

THIRD BLIND MAN.

Nobody goes toward the sea like that at his *t* age!

SECOND BLIND MAN,

Are we near the sea?

THE OLD BLIND WOMAN.

Yes; keep still a moment; you will hear it.

Murmur of a sea, near by and very calm, against the cliffs.

SECOND BLIND MAN.

I hear only the three old women praying.

THE VERY OLD BLIND WOMAN.

Listen well; you will hear it across their prayers.

SECOND BLIND MAN.

Yes; I hear something not far from us.

THE VERY OLD BLIND MAN.

It was asleep; one would say that it awaked.

FIRST BLIND MAN.

He was wrong to bring us here; I do not like to hear that noise.

THE VERY OLD BLIND MAN.

You know quite well the Island is not large. It can be heard whenever one goes outside the Asylum close.

SECOND BLIND MAN.

I never listened to it.

THIRD BLIND MAN.

It seems close beside us to-day; I do not like to hear it so near.

SECOND BLIND MAN.

No more do I; besides, we did n't ask to go out from the Asylum.

THIRD BLIND MAN.

We have never come so far as this; it was needless to bring us so far.

THE VERY OLD BLIND WOMAN.

The weather was very fine this morning; he wanted to have us enjoy the last sunny days, before shutting us up all winter in the Asylum.

FIRST BLIND MAN.

But I prefer to stay in the Asylum.

THE VERY OLD BLIND WOMAN.

He said also that we ought to know something of the little Island we live on. He himself had never been all over it; there is a mountain that no one has climbed, valleys one fears to go down into, and caves into which no one has ever yet penetrated. Finally he said we must not always wait for the sun under the vaulted roof of the dormitory; he wished to lead us as far as the seashore. He has gone there alone.

THE VERY OLD BLIND MAN.

He is right. We must think of living.

FIRST BLIND MAN.

But there is nothing to see outside!

SECOND BLIND MAN.

Are we in the sun, now?

THIRD BLIND MAN.

Is the sun still shining?

SIXTH BLIND MAN.

I think not: it seems very late.

SECOND BLIND MAN.

What time is it?

THE OTHERS.

I do not know. — Nobody knows.

SECOND BLIND MAN.

Is it light still? *To the sixth blind man,* — Where are you? — How is it, you who can see a little, how is it?

SIXTH BLIND MAN.

I think it is very dark; when there is sunlight, I see a blue line under my eyelids. I did see one, a long while ago; but now, I no longer perceive anything.

FIRST BLIND MAN.

For my part, I know it is late when I am hungry: and I am hungry.

THIRD BLIND MAN.

Look up at the sky; perhaps you will see something there!

All lift their heads skyward, with the exception of the three who were born blind, who continue to look upon the ground SIXTH BLIND MAN.

J do not know whether we are under the sky. FIRST BLIND MAN.

The voice echoes as if we were in a cavern.

THE VERY OLD BLIND MAN.

I think, rather, that it echoes so because it is evening.

THE YOUNG BLIND GIRL.

It seems to me that I feel the moonlight on my hands.

THE VERY OLD BLIND WOMAN.

I believe there are stars; I hear them.

THE YOUNG BLIND GIRL.

So do I.

FIRST BLIND MAN.

I hear no noise.

SECOND BLIND MAN.

I hear only the noise of our breathing.

THE VERY OLD BLIND MAN.

I believe the women are right.

FIRST BLIND MAN.

I never heard the stars.

THE TWO OTHERS WHO WERE BORN BLIND.

Nor we, either.

A flight of night birds alights suddenly in the foliage SECOND BLIND MAN.

Listen! listen! — what is up there above us? — Do you hear?

THE VERY OLD BLIND MAN.

Something has passed between us and the sky!

SKTH BLIND MAN.

There is something stirring over our heads; but we cannot reach there!

FIRST BLIND MAN.

I do not recognize that noise. — I should like to go back to the Asylum.

SECOND BLIND MAN.

We ought to know where we are!

SLXTH BLIND MAN.

I have tried to get up; there is nothing but thorns about me; I dare not stretch out my hands.

THIRD BLIND MAN.

We ought to know where we are!

THE VERY OLD BLIND MAN.

We cannot know!

SIXTH BLIND MAN.

We must be very far from the house. I no longer understand any of the noises.

THIRD BLIND MAN.

For a long time I have smelled the odor of dead leaves — SIXTH BLIND MAN.

Is there any of us who has seen the Island in the past, and can tell us where we are?

THE VERY OLD BLIND WOMAN.

We were all blind when we came here.

FIRST BLIND MAN.

We have never seen.

SECOND BLIND MAN.

Let us not alarm ourselves needlessly. He will come back soon; let us wait a little longer. But in the future, we will not go out any more with him.

THE VERY OLD BLIND MAN.

We cannot go out alone.

FIRST BLIND MAN.

We will not go out at all. I had rather not go out.

SECOND BLIND MAN.

We had no desire to go out. Nobody asked him to.

THE VERY OLD BLIND WOMAN.

It was a feast-day in the Island; we always go out on the great holidays.

THIRD BLIND MAN.

He tapped me on the shoulder while I was still asleep, saying: "Rise, rise; it is time, the sun is shining!" — Is it? I had not perceived it. I never saw the sun.

THE VERY OLD BLIND MAN. / have seen the sun, when I was very young. THE VERY OLD BLIND WOMAN.

So have I; a very long time ago; when I was a child; but I hardly remember it any longer.

THIRD BLIND MAN.

Why does he want us to go out every time the sun shines? Who can tell the difference? I never, know whether I take a walk at noon or at midnight.

SIXTH BLIND MAN.

I had rather go out at noon; I guess vaguely then at a great white light, and my eyes make great efforts to open.

THIRD BLIND MAN.

I prefer to stay in the refectory, near the seacoal fire; there was a big fire this morning..,. SECOND BLIND MAN.

He could take us into the sun in the courtyard. There the walls are a shelter; you cannot go out when the gate is shut, — I always shut it. — Why are you touching my left elbow?

FIRST BLIND MAN.

I have not touched you. I can't reach you.

SECOND BLIND MAN.

I tell you somebody touched my elbow!

FIRST BLIND MAN.

It was not any of us.

SECOND BLIND MAN.

I should like to go away.

THE VERY OLD BLIND WOMAN.

My God! my God! Tell us where we

are!

FIRST BLIND MAN.

We cannot wait for eternity.

A clock, very far away, strikes twelve slowly THE VERY OLD BLIND WOMAN.

Oh, how far we are from the asylum!

THE VERY OLD BLIND MAN.

It is midnight.

SECOND BLIND MAN.

It is noon. — Does any one know? — Speak!

SIXTH BLIND MAN.

I do not know, but I think we are in the dark.

FIRST BLIND MAN.

I don't know any longer where I am; we slept too long — SECOND BLIND MAN.

I am hungry.

THE OTHERS.

We are hungry and thirsty.

SECOND BLIND MAN.

Have we been here long?

THE VERY OLD BLIND WOMAN.

It seems as if I had been here centuries!

SIXTH BLIND MAN.

I begin to understand where we are....

THIRD BLIND MAN.

We ought to go toward the side where it struck midnight....

All at once the night birds scream exultingly in the darkness FIRST BLIND MAN.

Do you hear? — Do you hear?

SECOND BLIND MAN.

We are not alone here!

THIRD BLIND MAN.

I suspected something a long while ago: we are overheard. — Has he come back?

FIRST BLIND MAN.

I don't know what it is: it is above us.

SECOND BLIND MAN.

Did the others hear nothing? — You are always silent!

THE VERY OLD BLIND MAN.

We are listening still.

THE YOUNG BLIND GIRL.

I hear wings about me!

THE VERY OLD BLIND WOMAN.

My God! my God! Tell us where we are!

SIXTH BLIND MAN.

I begin to understand where we are....
The Asylum is on the other side of the great river; we crossed the old bridge.

He led us to the north of the Island. We are not far from the river, and perhaps we shall hear it if we listen a moment... . We must go as far as the water's edge, if he does not come back.... There, night and day, great ships pass, and the sailors will perceive us on the banks. It is possible that we are in the wood that surrounds the lighthouse; but I do not know the way out.... Will any one follow me?

FIRST BLIND MAN.

Let us remain seated! — Let us wait, let us wait. We do not know in what direction' the great river is, and there are marshes all about the Asylum. Let us wait, let us wait.... He will return.... he must return!

SIXTH BLIND MAN.

Does any one know by what route we came here? He explained it to us as he walked.

FIRST BLIND MAN.

I paid no attention to him.

SLXTH BLIND MAN.

Did any one listen to him?

THIRD BLIND MAN. We must listen to him in the future. SIXTH BLIND MAN.

Were any of us born on the Island?

THE VERY OLD BLIND MAN.

You know very well we came from elsewhere.

THE VERY OLD BLIND WOMAN.

We came from the other side of the sea.

FIRST BLIND MAN.

I thought I should die on the voyage.

SECOND BLIND MAN.

So did I; we came together.

THIRD BLIND MAN.

We are all three from the same parish.

FIRST BLIND MAN.

They say you can see it from here, on a clear day, — toward the north. It has no steeple.

THIRD BLIND MAN.

We came by accident.

THE VERY OLD BLIND WOMAN.

I come from another direction....

SECOND BLIND MAN.

From where?

THE VERY OLD BLIND WOMAN.

I dare no longer dream of it.... I hardly remember any longer when I speak of it. ... It was too long ago.... It was colder there than here....

THE YOUNG BLIND GIRL.

I come from very far....

FIRST BLIND MAN.

Well, from where?

THE YOUNG BLIND GIRL.

I could not tell you. How would you have me explain! — It is too far from here; it is beyond the sea. I come from a great country.... I could only make you understand by signs: and we no longer see.... I have wandered too long.... But I have seen the sunlight and the water and the fire, mountains, faces, and strange flowers.... There are none such on this Island; it is too gloomy and too cold... . I have never recognized their perfume since I saw them last.... And I have seen my parents and my sisters.... I was too young then to know where I was.... I still played by the seashore.... But oh, how I remember having seen!... One day I saw the snow on a mountain-top... I began to distinguish the unhappy...

FIRST BLIND MAN.

What do you mean?

THE YOUNG BLIND GIRL.

I distinguish them yet at times by their voices.... I have memories which are clearer when I do not think upon them.. ..

FIRST BLIND MAN.

I have no memories.

A flight of large migratory birds pass clamor.ously, above the trees THE VERY OLD BLIND MAN.

Something is passing again across the sky!

SECOND BLIND MAN.

Why did you come here?

THE VERY OLD BLIND MAN.

Of whom do you ask that?

SECOND BLIND MAN.

Of our young sister.

THE YOUNG BLIND GIRL.

I was told he could cure me. He told me I would see some day; then I could leave the Island....

FIRST BLIND MAN.

We all want to leave the Island!

SECOND BLIND MAN.

We shall stay here always.

THIRD BLIND MAN.

He is too old; he will not have time to cure us.

THE YOUNG BLIND GIRL.

My lids are shut, but I feel that my eyes

are alive....

FIRST BLIND MAN.

Mine are open.

SECOND BLIND MAN.

I sleep with my eyes open.

THIRD BLIND MAN.

Let us not talk of our eyes!

SECOND BLIND MAN.

It is not long since you came, is it?

THE VERY OLD BLIND MAN.

One evening at prayers I heard a voice on the women's side that I did not recognize; and I knew by your voice that you were very young.... I would have liked to see you, to hear you....

FIRST BLIND MAN.

I did n't perceive anything.

SECOND BLIND MAN.

He gave us no warning.

SIXTH BLIND MAN.

They say you are beautiful as a woman who comes from very far.

THE YOUNG BLIND GIRL.

I have never seen myself.

THE VERY OLD BLIND MAN.

We have never seen each other. We ask and ve reply; we live together, we are always together, but we know not what we are!... In vain we touch each other with both hands; the eyes learn more than the hands....

SIXTH BLIND MAN.

I see your shadows sometimes, when you are in the sun.

THE VERY OLD BLIND MAN.

We have never seen the house in which we live; in vain we feel the walls and the windows; we do not know where we live!...

THE VERY OLD BLIND WOMAN.

They say it is an old chateau, very gloomy and very wretched, where no light is ever seen except in the tower where the priest has his room.

FIRST BLIND MAN.

There is no need of light for those who do not see.

SIXTH BLIND MAN.

When I tend the flock, in the neighborhood of the Asylum, the sheep return of themselves when they see at nightfall that light in the tower... They have never misled me.

THE VERY OLD BLIND MAN.

Years and years we have been together,

and we have never seen each other! You would say we were forever alone!... To love, one must see.

THE VERY OLD BLIND WOMAN.

I dream sometimes that I see...

THE VERY OLD BLIND MAN.

I see only in my dreams...

FIRST BLIND MAN.

I do not dream, usually, except at midnight.

SECOND BLIND MAN.

Of what can one dream where the hands are motionless?

A flurry of wind shakes the forest, and the leaves fall, thick and gloomily.

FIFTH BLIND MAN.

Who touched my hands?

FIRST BLIND MAN.

Something is falling about us!

THE VERY OLD BLIND MAN.

That comes from above; I don't know what it is...

FIFTH BLIND MAN.

Who touched my hands? — I was asleep; let me sleep!

THE VERY OLD BLIND MAN.

Nobody touched your hands.

FIFTH BLIND MAN.

Who took my hands? Answer loudly; I am a little hard of hearing...

THE VERY OLD BLIND MAN.

We do not know ourselves.

FIFTH BLIND MAN.

Has some one come to give us warning?

FIRST BLIND MAN.

It is useless to reply; he hears nothing.

THIRD BLIND MAN.

It must be admitted, the deaf are very unfortunate.

THE VERY OLD BLIND MAN.

I am weary of staying seated.

SIXTH BLIND MAN.

I am weary of staying here.

SECOND BLIND MAN.

It seems to me we are so far from one another.... Let us try to get a little nearer together, — it is beginning to get cold...
.

THIRD BLIND MAN.

I dare not rise! We had better stay where we are.

THE VERY OLD BLIND MAN.

We do not know what there may be among us.

SIXTH BLIND MAN.

I think both my hands are in blood; I would like to stand up.

THIRD BLIND MAN.

You are leaning toward me, — I hear you.

The blind madwoman rubs her eyes violently, groaning and turning obstinately toward the motionless priest

FIRST BLIND MAN.

I hear still another noise....

THE VERY OLD BLIND WOMAN.

I think it is our unfortunate sister rubbing her eyes.' SECOND BLIND MAN.

She is never doing anything else; I hear her every night.

THIRD BLIND MAN.

She is mad; she never speaks.

THE VERY OLD BLIND WOMAN.

She has never spoken since she had her child.... She seems always to be afraid...
.

THE VERY OLD BLIND MAN.

You are not afraid here, then?

FIRST BUND MAN.

Who?

THE VERY OLD BLIND MAN.

All the rest of us.

THE VERY OLD BLIND WOMAN.

Yes, yes; we are afraid.

THE YOUNG BLIND GIRL.

We have been afraid for a long time.

FIRST BLIND MAN.

Why did you ask that?

THE VERY OLD BLIND MAN.

I do not know why I asked it.... There is something here I do not understand.... It seems to me I hear weeping all at once among us....

FIRST BLIND MAN.

There is no need to fear; I think it is the madwoman.

THE VERY OLD BLIND MAN.

There is something else beside.... I am sure there is something else beside.... It is not that alone that makes me afraid.

THE VERY OLD BLIND WOMAN.

She always weeps when she is going to give suck to her child.

FIRST BLIND MAN.

She is the only one that weeps so.

THE VERY OLD BLIND WOMAN.

They say she sees still at times.

FIRST BLIND MAN.

You do not hear the others weep.

THE VERY OLD BLIND MAN.

To weep, one must see.

THE YOUNG BLIND GIRL.

I smell an odor of flowers about us.

FIRST BLIND MAN.

I smell only the smell of the earth.

THE YOUNG BLIND GIRL.

There are flowers, — there are flowers, about us.

SECOND BLIND MAN.

I smell only the smell of the earth.

THE VERY OLD BLIND WOMAN.

I caught the perfume of flowers in the wind....

THIRD BLIND MAN.

I smell only the smell of the earth.

THE VERY OLD BLIND MAN.

I believe the women are right.

SIXTH BLIND MAN.

Where are they? — I will go pluck them.

THE YOUNG BLIND GIRL.

At your right. Rise!

The sixth blind man rises slowly and advances groping, and stumbling against the bushes and trees, toward the asphodels, which he breaks and crushes on his way.

THE YOUNG BLIND GIRL.

I hear you breaking the green stalks. Stop! stop!

FIRST BLIND MAN.

Don't worry yourselves about flowers, but think of getting home.

SDCTH BLIND MAN.

I no longer dare return on my steps.

THE YOUNG BLIND GIRL.

You need not return. — Wait. — *She rises.* Oh, how cold the earth is! It is going to freeze. — *She advances without hesitation toward the strange, pale asphodels; but she is stopped, in the neighborhood of the flowers, by the up-rooted tree and the fragments of rock.* They are here. — I cannot reach them; they are on your side.

SIXTH BLIND MAN.

I believe I am plucking them.

He plucks the scattered flowers, gropingly, and offers them to her; the night birds fly away.

THE YOUNG BLIND GIRL.

It seems to me I saw these flowers in the old days.... I no longer know their name.... Alas, how sickly they are, and how soft the stems are! I hardly recog-

nize them.... I think it is the flower of the dead.

She twines the asphodels in her hair.

THE VERY OLD BLIND MAN.

I hear the noise of your hair.

THE YOUNG BLIND GIRL.

It is the flowers.

THE VERY OLD BLIND MAN.

We shall not see you....

THE YOUNG BLIND GIRL.

I shall not see myself, any more.... I am cold.

At this moment the wind rises in the forest, and the sea roars suddenly and with violence against cliffs very near.

FIRST BLIND MAN.

It thunders!

SECOND BLIND MAN.

I think there is a storm rising.

THE VERY OLD BLIND WOMAN.

I think it is the sea.

THIRD BLIND MAN.

The sea? — Is it the sea?— But it is hardly two steps from us! — It is at our feet! I hear it all about me! — It must be something else!

THE YOUNG BLIND GIRL.

I hear the noise of breakers at my feet.

FIRST BLIND MAN.

I think it is the wind in the dead leaves.

THE VERY OLD BLIND MAN.

I think the women are right.

THIRD BLIND MAN.

It will come here!

FIRST BLIND MAN.

What direction does the wind come from?

SECOND BLIND MAN.

It comes from the sea.

THE VERY OLD BLIND MAN.

It always comes from the sea. The sea surrounds us on all sides. It cannot come from anywhere else....

FIRST BLIND MAN.

Let us not keep on thinking of the sea!

SECOND BLIND MAN.

We must think of it. It will reach us soon.

FIRST BLIND MAN.

You do not know if it be the sea.

SECOND BLIND MAN.

I hear its surges as if I could dip both hands in them. We cannot stay here! It is perhaps all about us.

THE VERY OLD BLIND MAN.

Where would you go?

SECOND BLIND MAN.

No matter where! no matter where! I will not hear this noise of waters any longer! Let us go! Let us go!

THIRD BLIND MAN.

I think I hear something else. — Listen!

A sound of footfalls is heard, hurried and fat away, in the dead leaves.

FIRST BLIND MAN.

There is something coming this way.

SECOND BLIND MAN.

He is coming! He is coming! He is coming back!

THIRD BLIND MAN.

He is coming with little quick steps, like a little child.

SECOND BLIND MAN.

Let us make no complaints to him to-day.

THE VERY OLD BLIND WOMAN.

I believe that is not the step of a man!

A great dog enters in the forest, and passes in front of the blind folk. — Silence.

FIRST BLIND MAN.

Who's there? — Who are you? — Have pity on us, we have been waiting so long!... *The dog stops, and coming to the blind man, puts his fore paws on his knees.* Oh, oh, what have you put on my knees? What is it?... Is it an animal? — I believe it is a dog.... Oh, oh, it is the dog, it is the Asylum dog! Come here, sir, come here! He comes to save us! Come here! come here, sir!

THE OTHERS.

Come here, sir! come here!

FIRST BLIND MAN.

He has come to save us! He has followed our tracks all the way! He is licking my hands as if he had just found me after centuries! He howls for joy! He is going to die for joy! Listen, listen!

THE OTHERS.

Come here! Come here!

THE VERY OLD BLIND MAN.

Perhaps he is running ahead of somebody...

FIRST BLIND MAN.

No, no, he is alone. — I hear nothing coming. — We need no other guide; there is none better. He will lead us wherever we want to go; he will obey us...

THE VERY OLD BLIND WOMAN.

I dare not follow him....

THE YOUNG BLIND GIRL.

Nor I.

FIRST BLIND MAN.

Why not? His sight is better than ours.

SECOND BLIND MAN.

Don't listen to the women!

THIRD BLIND MAN.

I believe there is a change in the sky. I breathe freely. The air is pure now...

THE VERY OLD BLIND WOMAN.

It is the sea wind passing about us.

SIXTH BLIND MAN.

It seems to me it is getting lighter; I believe the sun is rising...

THE VERY OLD BLIND WOMAN.

I believe it is getting colder....

FIRST BLIND MAN.

We are going to find our way again. He is dragging me!... he is dragging me. He is drunk with joy! — I can no longer hold him back!... Follow me, follow me. We are going back to the house!...

He rises, dragged by the dog, who leads him to the motionless priest, and stops.

THE OTHERS.

Where are you? Where are you? — Where are you going? — Take care!

FIRST BLIND MAN.

Wait, wait! Do not follow me yet; I will come back... He is stopping. — What is the matter with him? — Oh, oh, I touched something very cold!

SECOND BLIND MAN.

What are you saying? — We can hardly hear your voice any longer.

FIRST BLIND MAN.

I have touched — I believe I am touching a face!

THIRD BLIND MAN.

What are you saying? — We hardly understand you any longer. What is the matter with you? — Where are you? — Are you already so far away?

FIRST BLIND MAN.

Oh, oh, oh! — I do not know yet what it is. — There is a dead man in the midst of us.

THE OTHERS.

A dead man in the midst of us? — Where are you? Where are you?

FIRST BLIND MAN.

There is a dead man among us, I tell you! Oh, oh, I touched a dead man's face! — You are sitting beside a dead man! One of us must have died suddenly. Why don't you speak, so that I may know who are still alive? Where are you? — Answer! answer, all of you!

The blind folk reply in turn, with the exception of the madwoman and the deaf man. The three old women have ceased their prayers.

FIRST BLIND MAN.

I no longer distinguish your voices... You all speak alike!... Your voices are all trembling.

THIRD BLIND MAN.

There are two that have not answered... Where are they?

He touches with his stick the fifth blind man.

FIFTH BLIND MAN.

Oh! oh! I was asleep; let me sleep!

SIXTH BLIND MAN.

It is not he. — Is it the madwoman?

THE VERY OLD BLIND WOMAN.

She is sitting beside me; I can hear that she is alive...

FIRST BLIND MAN.

I believe... I believe it is the priest! — He is standing up! Come, come, come!

SECOND BLIND MAN.

He is standing up?

THIRD BLIND MAN.

Then he is not dead!

THE VERY OLD BLIND MAN.

Where is he?

SIXTH BLIND MAN.

Let us go see!

They all rise, with the exception of the madwoman and the fifth blind man, and advance, groping, toward the dead

SECOND BLIND MAN.

Is he here? — Is it he?

THIRD BLIND MAN.

Yes, yes, I recognize him.

FIRST BLIND MAN.

My God) my God! what will become of us?

THE VERY OLD BLIND WOMAN.

Father! father! — Is it you? Father, what has happened? — What is the matter? — Answer us! — We are all about you. Oh! oh! oh!

THE VERY OLD BLIND MAN.

Bring some water; perhaps he still lives.

SECOND BLIND MAN.

Let us try... He might perhaps be able to take us back to the Asylum...

THIRD BLIND MAN.

It is useless; I no longer hear his heart. — He is cold.

FIRST BLIND MAN.

He died without speaking a word.

THIRD BLIND MAN.

He ought to have forewarned us.

SECOND BLIND MAN.

Oh! how old he was!... This is the first time I ever touched his face...

THIRD BLIND MAN. *Feeling the corpse.* ' He is taller than we. SECOND BLIND MAN.

His eyes are wide open. He died with his hands clasped.

FIRST BLIND MAN.

It was unreasonable to die so...

SECOND BLIND MAN.

He is not standing up, he is sitting on a stone.

THE VERY OLD BLIND WOMAN.

My God! my God! I did not dream of such a thing!... such a thing!... He has been sick such a long time... He must have suffered to-day... Oh, oh, oh! — He never complained; he only pressed our hands... One does not always understand... Qne never understands!... Let us go pray about him; go down on your knees...

The women kneel, moaning.

FIRST BLIND MAN.

I dare not go down on my knees.

SECOND BLIND MAN.

You cannot tell what you might kneel on here.

THIRD BLIND MAN.

Was he ill?... He did not tell us...

SECOND BLIND MAN.

I heard him muttering in a low voice as he went away. I think he was speaking to our young sister. What did he say?

FIRST BLIND MAN.

She will not answer.

SECOND BLIND MAN.

Will you no longer answer us? — Where are you, I say? — Speak.

THE VERY OLD BLIND WOMAN.

You made him suffer too much; you have made him die.... You would not go on; you would sit down on the stones of the road to eat; you have grumbled all day... I heard him sigh... He lost heart...

FIRST BLIND MAN.

Was he ill? Did you know it?

THE VERY OLD BLIND MAN.

We knew nothing... We never saw him. ... When did we ever know anything behind our poor dead eyes?... He never complained. Now it is too late... I have seen three die... but never in this way!... Now it is our turn.

FIRST BLIND MAN.

It was not I that made him suffer. — I said nothing.

SECOND BLIND MAN.

No more did I. We followed him without saying anything.

THIRD BLIND MAN.

He died, going after water for the madwoman.

FIRST BLIND MAN.

What are we going to do now? Where shall we go?

THIRD BLIND MAN.

Where is the dog?

FIRST BLIND MAN.

Here; he will not go away from the dead man.

THIRD BLIND MAN.

Drag him away! Take him off, take him off!

FIRST BLIND MAN.

He will not leave the dead man.

SECOND BLIND MAN.

We cannot wait beside a dead man. We cannot die here in the dark.

THIRD BLIND MAN.

Let us remain together; let us not scatter; let us hold one another by the hand; let us all sit on this stone... Where are the others?... Come here, come, come!

THE VERY OLD BLIND MAN.

Where are you?

THIRD BLIND MAN.

Here; I am here. Are we all together? — Come nearer me. — Where are your hands? — Jt is very cold, THE YOUNG BLIND GIRL.

Oh, how cold your hands are!

THIRD BLIND MAN.

What are you doing?

THE YOUNG BLIND GIRL.

I was putting my hands on my eyes thought I was going to see all at once..

FIRST BLIND MAN.

Who is weeping so?

THE VERY OLD BLIND WOMAN.

It is the madwoman sobbing.

FIRST BLIND MAN.

And yet she does not know the truth.

THE VERY OLD BLIND MAN.

I think we are going to die here.

THE VERY OLD BLIND WOMAN.

Perhaps some one will come...

THE VERY OLD BLIND MAN.

Who else would come?...

THE VERY OLD BLIND WOMAN.

I do not know, FIRST BLIND MAN.

I think the nuns will come out from the Asylum...

THE VERY OLD BLIND WOMAN.

They do not go out after dark.

THE YOUNG BLIND GIRL.

They never go out.

SECOND BLIND MAN.

I think the men at the great lighthouse will perceive us...

THE VERY OLD BLIND MAN.

They never come down from their tower.

THIRD BLIND MAN.

They will see us, perhaps....

THE VERY OLD BLIND WOMAN.

They look always out to sea.

THIRD BUND MAN.

It is cold.

THE VERY OLD BLIND MAN.

Listen to the dead leaves. I believe it is freezing.

THE YOUNG BLIND GIRL.

Oh! how hard the earth is!

THIRD BLIND MAN.

I hear on my left a sound I do not understand.

THE VERY OLD BLIND MAN.

It is the sea moaning against the rocks.

THIRD BLIND MAN.

I thought it was the women.

THE VERY OLD BLIND WOMAN.

I hear the ice breaking under the surf.

FIRST BLIND MAN.

Who is shivering so? It shakes everybody on the stone.

SECOND BLIND MAN.

I can no longer open my hands.

THE VERY OLD BLIND MAN.

I hear again a sound I do not understand.

FIRST BLIND MAN.

Who is shivering so among us? It shakes the stone.

THE VERY OLD BLIND MAN.

I think it is a woman.

THE VERY OLD BLIND WOMAN.

I think the madwoman is shivering the hardest.

THIRD BLIND MAN.

We do not hear her child.

THE VERY OLD BLIND WOMAN.

I think he is still nursing.

THE VERY OLD BLIND MAN.

He is the only one who can see where we are!

FIRST BLIND MAN.

I hear the north wind.

SIXTH BLIND MAN.

I think there are no more stars; it is going to snow.

SECOND BLIND MAN.

Then we are lost!

THIRD BLIND MAN.

If any one sleeps, he must be aroused.

THE VERY OLD BLIND MAN.

Nevertheless, I am sleepy.

A sudden gust sweeps the dead leaves around in a whirlwind THE YOUNG BLIND GIRL.

Do you hear the dead leaves? — I believe some one is coming toward us, SECOND BLIND MAN.

It is the wind; listen!

THIRD BLIND MAN.

No one will ever come.

THE VERY OLD BLIND MAN.

The great cold will come...

THE YOUNG BLIND GIRL.

I hear walking far off.

FIRST BLIND MAN.

I hear only the dead leaves.

THE YOUNG BLIND GIRL.

I hear walking far away from us.

SECOND BLIND MAN.

I hear only the north wind.

THE YOUNG BLIND GIRL.

I tell you, some one is coming toward us.

THE VERY OLD BLIND WOMAN.

I hear a sound of very slow footsteps.

THE VERY OLD BLIND MAN.

I believe the women are right.

It begins to snow in great flakes FIRST BLIND MAN.

Oh, oh! what is it falling so cold upon my hands?

SIXTH BLIND MAN.

It is snowing.

FIRST BLIND MAN.

Let us press close to one another.

THE YOUNG BLIND GIRL.

No, but listen! The sound of footsteps!

THE VERY OLD BLIND WOMAN.

For God's sake, keep still an instant.

THE YOUNG BLIND GIRL.

They come nearer! they come nearer! listen!

Here the child of the blind madwoman begins suddenly to wail in the darkness.

THE VERY OLD BLIND MAN.

The child is crying.

THE YOUNG BLIND GIRL.

He sees! he sees! He must see something if he cries. *She seizes the child in her arms and advances in the direction from which the sound of footsteps seems to come. The other women follow her anxiously and surround her.* I am going to meet him.

THE VERY OLD BLIND MAN.

Take care.

THE YOUNG BLIND GIRL.

Oh, how he cries! — What is the matter with him? — Don't cry. — Don't be afraid; there is nothing to frighten you, we are here; we are all about you. — What do you see?— Don't be afraid at all. — Don't cry so! — What do you see? — Tell me, what do you see?

THE VERY OLD BLIND WOMAN.

The sound of footsteps draws nearer and nearer: listen, listen!

THE VERY OLD BLIND MAN.

I hear the rustling of a gown against the dead leaves.

SIXTH BLIND MAN.

Is it a woman?

THE VERY OLD BLIND MAN.

Is it a noise of footsteps?

FIRST BLIND MAN.

Can it be perhaps the sea in the dead leaves?

THE YOUNG BLIND GIRL.

No, no! They are footsteps, they are footsteps, they are footsteps!

THE VERY OLD BLIND WOMAN.

We shall know soon. Listen to the dead leaves.

THE YOUNG BLIND GIRL.

I hear them, I hear them almost beside us; listen, listen! — What do you see? What do you see?

THE VERY OLD BLIND WOMAN.

Which way is he looking?

THE YOUNG BLIND GIRL.

He keeps following the sound of the steps. — Look, look! When I turn him away, he turns back to see... He sees, he sees, he sees!.— He must see something strange!

The Very Old Blind Woman *steppingforward.* Lift him above us, so that he may see better.

THE YOUNG BLIND GIRL.

Stand back, stand back. *She raises the child above the group of blind folk.* — The footsteps have stopped amongst us.

THE VERY OLD BLIND WOMAN.

They are here! They are in the midst of us 1...

THE YOUNG BLIND GIRL.

Who are you? *Silence.* THE VERY OLD BLIND WOMAN.

Have pity on us!

Silence. — The child weeps more desperately.

Persons.

The Old King.

The Old Queen.

The Prince.

The Seven Princesses.

A Messenger.

Chorus Of Sailors.

The Seven Princesses.

A spacious hall of marble, with laurel, lavender, and lilies in porcelain vases. A flight of seven white marble steps divides the whole hall lengthwise, and seven princesses, in white gowns and with bare arms, lie sleeping on these steps, which are-furnished with cushions of pale silk. A silver lamp shines on their sleep. At the back of the hall, a door with powerful bolts. To the right and left of this door large windows whose panes reach down to the level of the tiles. Behind these windows, a terrace. The sun is just setting, and through the panes a dark, marshy country is seen, with pools and forests of oaks and pines. Vertically with one of the windows, between huge willows, a gloomy canal without a bend, on the horizon of which a large manof-war approaches.

The old King, the old Queen and the Messenger come forward upon the terrace and watch the approach of the manof-war.

THE QUEEN.

It comes with all sails set....

THE KING.

I do not see it well through the fog.

QUEEN.

They are rowing — they are all rowing. ... I believe they are going to come to the very windows of the chateau.... You would say it had a thousand feet... the sails touch the branches of the willows....

KING.

It looks larger than the canal....

QUEEN.

They are stopping....

KING.

I do not know how they will be able to go back....

QUEEN.

They are stopping... they are stopping. They are coming to anchor.... They are making fast to the willows.... Oh! oh! I believe the prince is coming down —...

KING.

Just look at the swans.... They are going to meet him.... They are going to see what it is....

QUEEN.

Are they still asleep?

They come and look through the windows into the hall.

KING.

Let us wake them.... I told you so a long while ago; they must be wakened....

QUEEN.

Let us wait till he come.... It is too late now.... He is here; he is here! — My God, my God! what shall we do? — I dare not! I dare not!... They are too ill....

KING.

Shall I open the door?

QUEEN.

No, no! Wait! Let us wait! — Oh, how they sleep! how they still sleep!... They do not know he has come back — they do not know he is here.... I dare not wake them... the physician forbade it... let us not wake them.... Let us not wake them yet.... Oh, oh! I hear a sound of footsteps on the bridge....

KING.

He is here! He is here!... He is at the foot of the terrace!...

They leave the window. QUEEN.

Where is he? Where is he? — Is it he? — I should no longer know him!... Yes, yes; I should know him still! Oh, how tall he is! how tall he is! He is at the foot of the steps!... Marcellus! Marcellus! Is it you? Is it you? — Come up! come up! We are so old — we can no longer come down to you.... Come up! come up! come up!

KING.

Take care you do not fall!... the steps are very old... they all shake.... Take care!...

QUEEN.

Come up! come up! come up!

The Prince ascends to the terrace and throws himself in the arms of the King and Queen.

THE PRINCE.

My poor grandam! My poor grandfather!

They kiss. QUEEN.

Oh, how handsome you are!— How you have grown, my child! — How tall you are, my little Marcellus! — I do not see you well; my eyes are full of tears...
.

PRINCE.

Oh, my poor grandam, how white your hair is!... Oh, my poor grandfather, how white your beard is!...

KING.

We are poor little old people; our turn is coming....

PRINCE.

Grandfather, grandfather, why do you bend so?

KING.

I am always bent....

QUEEN.

We have waited for you so long!...

PRINCE.

Oh, my poor grandam, how you tremble this evening!...

QUEEN.

I always tremble so, my child....

PRINCE.

Oh, my poor grandfather! Oh, my poor grandam! I hardly know you any longer.
...

KING.

No more do I! no more do I! I no longer see very well....

QUEEN.

Where have you been so long, my child? — Oh, how tall you are!— You are taller than we!... There, there, I am weeping as if you were dead!

PRINCE.

Why do you receive me with tears in your eyes?

QUEEN.

No, no, it is not tears, my child.... It is not the same thing as tears.... Nothing has happened.... Nothing has happened.
...

PRINCE.

Where are my seven cousins?

QUEEN.

Here, here; listen, listen.... do not speak too loud; they sleep still; we must not speak of those who sleep...

PRINCE.

They sleep?... Are they still living, — all seven?...

QUEEN.

Yes, yes, yes; take care, take care.... They are asleep here; they are always asleep....

PRINCE.

They are always asleep?... What? what? what? — Do they —?... all seven! all seven!...

QUEEN.

Oh, oh, oh! what did you think?... what did you dare think, Marcellus, Marcellus? Take care! — They are here; come, look through the window... come, look. ... Quick, quick; come quick! It is time to see them....

They draw near the windows and lpok into the hall. A long silence.

PRINCE.

It is my seven cousins?... I do not see plainly....

QUEEN.

Yes, yes; they are all seven there on the steps.... Do you see them? Do you see them?

PRINCE.

I see only some white shadows....

QUEEN.

It is your seven cousins!... Do you see them in the mirrors?...

PRINCE.

It is my seven cousins?...

QUEEN.

Pray, look in the mirrors at the very end of the hall... you will see them; you will see them.... Come here, come here; you will see better, perhaps.

PRINCE.

I see! I see! I see! I see them, — all seven!... One, two, three *he hesitates a moment,* four, five, six, seven.... I hardly recognize them.... I do not recognize them at all.... Oh, how white they are, all seven!... Oh, how fair they are, all seven!... Oh, how pale they are, all seven!... But why do all the seven sleep?

QUEEN.

They always sleep.... They have slept here since noon.... They are so ill!... You can no longer wake them.... They did not know you were about to come.. .. We have not dared wake them.... We must wait.... They must awake of themselves.... They are not happy; it is not our fault.... We are too old, too old; everybody is too old for them. People are too old without knowing it....

PRINCE.

Oh, how beautiful they are! how beautiful they are!...

QUEEN.

They hardly live any longer since they have been here; — they have been here ever since their parents died.... It is too cold in this chateau.... They come from the warm countries.... They are alway seeking the sunshine; but there is almost none.... There was a little on the canal this morning; but the trees are too tall; there is too much shade; there is nothing but shade.... There are too many fogs, and the sky is never clear.... — Oh, how you look at them! — Do you see anything extraordinary?

PRINCE.

Oh, how pale they are, all seven!

QUEEN.

They are still fasting.... They could not stay in the garden any longer; the lawn dazzled them.... They have the fever.... They returned this noon holding one another by the hand.... They are so weak they can hardly walk alone now.... They shook with fever, — all seven. And no one knows what ails them.... They sleep here every day.

PRINCE.

They are strange.... Oh, oh, they are strange!... I dare no longer look at them. Is this their bedchamber?

QUEEN.

No, no; it is not their bedchamber....

You see plainly; there are no beds. Their seven little beds are above, — in the tower.... They are here, waiting for the night.

PRINCE.

I begin to make them out....

QUEEN.

Draw near, draw near; but do not touch the windows.... You will see better when the sun has set; it is too light still outside.... You will see better soon. Stand close to the window-panes; but make no noise....

PRINCE.

Oh, how light it is in the hall!...

QUEEN.

It will be lighter still when the night has come.... It is about to fall....

KING.

What is that about to fall?

QUEEN.

I spoke of the night. — Do you see anything?

PRINCE.

There is a great crystal vase upon a tripod....

QUEEN.

That is nothing; it is water; they are so thirsty when they wake!...

PRINCE.

But why is that lamp burning?

QUEEN.

They always light it. They knew they would sleep a long time. They lighted it this noon that they might not wake in the darkness.... They are afraid of the dark....

PRINCE.

They have grown tall!

QUEEN.

They are growing yet.... They are getting too tall.... It is perhaps that which makes them so ill.... Do you recognize them?

PRINCE.

I should recognize them, perhaps, if I saw them in broad daylight....

QUEEN.

You have played so often with them when they were little.... Open your eyes. ...

PRINCE.

I see plainly only their little bare feet....

KING. *L00king in at another window.* I cannot see in very clearly this evening..

.. PRINCE.

They are too far from us....

QUEEN.

There is something over the mirrors this evening; I do not see quite what it is....

PRINCE.

There is a mist over the window-panes.... I am going to see if I can wipe it away. ...

QUEEN.

No, no! do not touch the window! They would wake with a start! — It is on the inside; it is on the other side; it is the heat of the hall....

PRINCE.

Six of them I can make out very well; but there is one in the middle....

KING.

They all look alike; I only distinguish them by their necklaces of precious stones....

PRINCE.

There is one I cannot see well....

QUEEN.

Which do you like best?

PRINCE.

The one you cannot see well....

QUEEN.

Which? I am a little hard of hearing....

PRINCE.

The one you cannot see well....

KING.

Which one is it you cannot see well? I hardly see any of them.

PRINCE.

The one in the middle....

QUEEN.

I knew well you would see her only!...

PRINCE.

Who is it?

QUEEN.

You know well who it is; I need not tell you.

PRINCE.

It is Ursula?

QUEEN.

Why, yes; why, yes; why, yes! You know well it is Ursula! it is Ursula! It is Ursula, who has waited for you for seven years! all night long! all night long! all day long! all day long!... Do you recognize her?...

PRINCE.

I do not see her well; there is a shadow over her....

QUEEN.

Yes, there is a shadow over her; I do not know what it is....

PRINCE.

I think it is the shadow of a column.... I shall see her better soon, when the sun has wholly set....

QUEEN.

No, no; it is no shadow of the sun....

PRINCE.

We shall see if the shadow moves away. ...

KING.

I see what it is; it is the shadow of the lamp.

QUEEN.

She is lying differently from the others. ...

KING.

She sleeps more soundly, that is all....

PRINCE.

She sleeps like a little child....

KING.

Come to this window; you will see better, perhaps.

PRINCE. *Going to another window.* I see her no berter. It is the face I cannot see. ... QUEEN.

Come to this window; you will see better perhaps...., PRINCE.

Going to another window. I see her no better.... It is very difficult to se,e her. .... One would say she was hiding....

QUEEN.

The face is almost invisible....

PRINCE.

I see the body very well, but I do not make out the face.... I think it is entirely turned heavenward....

QUEEN.

But you look only at one!...

PRINCE. *Still looking.* She is taller than the others.... QUEEN.

But do not look always at the only one we cannot see.... There are six others!...

PRINCE.

I look at them, too.... Oh, how clearly one can see the others!...

QUEEN.

Do you recognize them?—There is Genevieve, — Helen, — and Christabel... and on the other side there is Magdalen, —. Clara, — and Claribel with the emeralds.... — Just see; I believe they are holding each other, all seven, by the hand.... They fell asleep, taking hold of hands.... Oh, oh! the little sisters!... You would say they were afraid of losing each other in their sleep.... My God, my God! I wish they would awake!.., PRINCE.

Yes, yes; let us wake them.... Will you let me wake them?...

QUEEN.

No, no; not yet, not yet.... Let us not look at them any more; come, do not look at them any more; they will suddenly have bad dreams.... I will look at them no more; I will look at them no more.... I might break the glass!... Let us not look at them any more, we should be frightened!... Come away, come away, to the foot of the terrace; we will talk of other things; we have so many things to say.... Come away, come away; they will be afraid if they turn over; they will be afraid if they see us at all the windows. *Ta the old* King. You too, you too; come away, do not glue your white beard to the panes so... you do not know how terrifying you are!... — For the love of God, do not stay, both of you, at the windows!... Oh, come away; come away, I tell you!... You do not know what is going to happen.... Come here, come here, turn away, turn away! Look the other way! Look the other way a moment!... They are ill, they are ill!... Let us go further away.... Let them sleep alone!...

PRINCE. _Turning._ What is the matter? —Why, what is the matter? — Oh, how dark it is without!... Where are you? J cannot find you..,, KING.

Wait a moment; you have the light of the hall in your eyes still.... I do not see either.... Come. We are here....

They leave the windows. PRINCE.

Oh, how dark it is in the fields!... Where are we?

KING.

The sun has set....

QUEEN.

Marcellus; why. did you not come sooner, Marcellus?

PRINCE.

The messenger has told you; I have thought only of coming....

QUEEN.

They have waited for you so many

years! They have been always in this marble hall; they have watched the canal day and night.... On sunny days they have gone on the other bank... there is a hill there, from which you can see further; you cannot see the sea; but you can see the rocks....

PRINCE.

What is that gleam under the trees?

'KING.

It is the canal by which you came; there is always a gleam on the water....

PRINCE.

Oh, how dark it is to-night! — I no longer know where I am; I am like a stranger here....

KING.

The sky is overcast suddenly....

PRINCE.

There is a breeze in the willows....

KING.

There is a breeze day and night in the willows; we are not far from the sea. — Listen; it rains already....

PRINCE.

One would say there was weeping about the chateau....

KING.

It is the rain falling on the water; it is a very gentle rain....

QUEEN.

One would say there was weeping in the sky....

PRINCE.

Oh, how the water sleeps between the walls I,,, QUEEN.

It always sleeps so; it is very old too. ...

PRINCE.

The swans have sought shelter under the bridge....

KING.

And here are peasants bringing home their flocks....

PRINCE.

They seem to me very old and very poor....

KING.

They are very poor; I am king of very poor people.... It is beginning to grow cold....

PRINCE.

What is there yonder, across the water?

KING.

Down there? — It was some flowers;

the cold has killed them....

At this moment, far off across the fields a monotonous song is heard, of which the refrain only can be distinguished, taken up in chorus at regular intervals.

FAR-AWAY VOICES.

The Atlantic! The Atlantic!

KING.

What is that?

PRINCE.

It is the sailors; — I think they are turning the ship; they are preparing to depart....

FAR-AWAY VOICES.

We shall return no more! We shall return no more!

QUEEN.

Already all its sails are set....

PRINCE.

They depart to-night.....

FAR-AWAY VOICES.

The Atlantic! The Atlantic!

KING.

Is it true that they will return no more?

PRINCE.

I do not know; perhaps it will not be the same ones....

FAR-AWAY VOICES.

We shall return no more! We shall return no more!

QUEEN.

You do not look happy, my child.

PRINCE.

I? — Why should I not be happy? — I came to see her and I have seen her.,. I can see her nearer if I will... I can sit by her side if I will.... Can I not open the doors and take her hand? I may kiss her when I will; I have only to wake her. Why should I be unhappy?

QUEEN.

You do not look happy, though!... I am nearly seventy-five years old now... and I have been waiting for you always!... It is not you, not you!... It is no longer you!...

She turns away her head and sobs

KING.

What is the matter? Why, what is the matter? Why do you weep all at once?

QUEEN.

It is nothing; it is nothing; — it is not I who weep.... Do not mind me; — one weeps often without reason; — I am so old to-day. — It is over....

PRINCE.

I shall look happier soon....

QUEEN.

Come, come; they are perhaps there with open eyes.... Give me your hand; lead me to the windows; let us go look in at the windows.,,, FAR-AWAY VOICES.

The Atlantic! The Atlantic!

They all return and look through the windows PRINCE.

I cannot see yet.... It is too light....

QUEEN.

There is something changed in the hall!...

KING.

I see nothing at all.

PRINCE.

It is brighter than before....

QUEEN.

It is not the same; there is something changed in the hall....

PRINCE.

My eyes are not yet used to the light....

QUEEN.

They are no longer all in the same position!...

PRINCE.

Yes, yes; I believe they have made a little movement.,,, QUEEN.

Oh, oh! Christabel and Claribel?... See, see!... They were holding Ursula by the hand.... They no longer hold their sister by the hand.... They have let go her hands.... They have turned the other way....

PRINCE.

They were on the point of waking....

QUEEN.

We have come too late! We have come too late!...

KING.

I see only the lilies by the windows: — they are closed....

PRINCE.

They know it is nightfall....

KING.

And yet there is a light there....

PRINCE.

She is holding one of her hands strangely....

QUEEN.

Who is?

PRINCE.

Ursula....

QUEEN.

What is that hand?... I did not see it just now....

PRINCE.

The others concealed it....

KING.

I do not know what you mean; I do not even see the mirrors....

QUEEN.

She will be hurt!... She will be hurt!... She cannot sleep so; it is not natural... I wish she would put down her hand a little. — My God, my God, grant that she put down that little hand!... Her little arm must ache there so long!...

PRINCE.

I see nothing to sustain it...

QUEEN.

I cannot see her sleep so... I never yet saw her sleep so.... It is not a good sign.. .. It is not a good sign!.... She will never be able to move her hand again....

KING.

There is no reason to be so disturbed.. .

PRINCE.

The others sleep more simply....

QUEEN.

How tight their eyes are shut! How tight their eyes are shut!... Oh, oh! the little sisters! the little sisters!... What shall we do? — Oh, what shall we do about it?...

KING.

Take care, do not speak so close to the windows....

QUEEN.

I am not so close as you think....

KING.

Your mouth is on the panes....

PRINCE.

I see something else — something very indistinct....

QUEEN.

So do I, so do I. There is something I am beginning to see.... It stretches out to the door....

PRINCE.

There is something on the marble slabs. ... It is not a shadow.... It cannot be a shadow.... I cannot be clear what it is.... It might be her hair....

QUEEN.

But why has she not bound up her hair?. .. All the others have bound up their hair.... Look....

PRINCE.

I tell you it is her hair!... It stirs.... Oh, her hair is beautiful!... It is not the hair of a sick woman....

QUEEN.

She does not arrange it so for sleeping.. .. You would say she had intended to go out.

PRINCE.

She said nothing to you?...

QUEEN.

She said this noon as she closed the door: "Above all, do not wake us." — Then I kissed her, not to see that she was sad....

PRINCE.

They will be cold with their little feet almost naked on the marble!

QUEEN.

Yes, yes; they will be cold! — Oh, do not look so eagerly! *To the* King. Nor you either! Nor you either! — Do not look every moment! Do not look all the time!.,— Let us not all look together!.. . They are not happy! They are not happy!...

KING.

What is it now, all at once? — Are you the only one that may see, pray? — Why, what is the matter with you this evening? — You are not reasonable any more... I do not understand you... Everybody else must look the other way; everybody else must shut their eyes.... But this concerns us as much as you, I think....

QUEEN.

Oh, I know it concerns you.... Do not speak so, for the love of God!... Oh, oh!. .. Do not look at me! Do not look at me just now!... My God, my God! how motionless they are!...

KING.

They will not wake to-night; we would do better to go and sleep too....

QUEEN.

Let us wait still; let us wait still.... We shall see perhaps what it is...

KING.

We cannot look forever through the windowpanes; something must be done.

...

PRINCE.

Perhaps we could wake them from here.

...

KING.

I am going to knock softly on the door.
QUEEN.
No, no! Never! Never!... Oh! No, not you, not you! You would knock too loud.... Take care! Oh, take care! They are afraid of everything... I will knock myself on the window, if it must be.... They must see who knocks.... Wait, wait....
She knocks very softly at the window.
PRINCE.
They do not wake....
KING.
I see nothing at all....
QUEEN.
I am going to knock a little louder....
She knocks again at the window.' They do not stir yet... *The* Queen *knocks again at the window.* —You would say the hall was full of cotton... — Are you sure this is sleep?—Perhaps they have fainted... I cannot see them breathe... *The* Queen *knocks again at another window*: Knock a little harder... Knock on the other panes! Oh, oh! these little panes are thick! *The* Queen *and the* Prince *knock anxiously with both hands.* How motionless they are! How motionless they are! — It is the heavy sleep of the sick... It is the sleep of fever, which will not go away... I want to see them near!... They do not hear the noise we make.... It is not a natural sleep.... It is not a healthy sleep... I dare not knock harder....
PRINCE. *Listening against the panes.* I do not hear the least noise....
A long silence.
QUEEN. *Her face against the panes and in a sudden burst of tears.* Oh, how they sleep! how they sleep!... My God, my God! deliver them, deliver them! — How their little hearts sleep! — Vou cannot hear their little hearts! — It is a fearful sleep! — Oh, oh! how fearful people are, asleep!... I am always afraid in their sleeping-room!... I no longer see their little souls!... Where then are their little souls!... They make me afraid! they make me afraid! — It is now that I see it!... How they sleep, the little sisters! Oh, how thev sleep, how they sleep!... I believe they will sleep forever!... My God, my God, I pity them!... They are not happy! they are not hap-

py!... Now I see it all!... Seven little souls all night!... Seven little helpless souls!... Seven little friendless souls!... Their mouths are wide open.... Seven little open mouths!... Oh, I am sure they are thirsty!... I am sure they are terribly thirsty!... And all their eyes shut!... Oh, how alone they are; all seven! all seven! all seven!... And how they sleep! How they _ sleep! — How they sleep, the little queens!... I am sure they do not sleep!... Oh, what a sleep! what a deep sleep!... Oh, wake the dear hearts! Wake the little queens!... Wake the little sisters! All the seven! all the seven!... I cannot bear to see them so any longer! My God, my God, I pity them! I pity them! And I dare not wake them!... Oh, the light is so faint!... so faint!... so faint. .. And I dare not wake them!... *She sobs desperately against the window.*J KING. What is the matter? — What is the matter now? — Come, come, look no longer; it is better not to see them.... Come, come, come. *He tries to take her away.* PRINCE.
Grandmother! grandmother!... What have you seen? what have you seen? — I have seen nothing.... There is nothing, there is nothing....
KING. *To the* Prince. It is nothing, it is nothing; do not mind her; it is old age, it is the night.... She is unnerved. — Women must weep. She weeps often in the night. *To the* Queen. J Come, come, come here.... You will fall! — Take care.... Lean on me.... Do not weep any more; do not weep any more, come.... *He kisses her tenderly* J It is nothing; they are sleeping.... We sleep, too.... We all sleep so.... Have you never seen any one sleep? QUEEN.
Never! Never as to-night! — Open the door! Open the door!... No one loves them enough!... No one can love them! — Open the door! Open the door!...
KING.
Yes; yes; we will open the door.... Be calm, be calm, — think no more of it; we will open it, we will open it. I ask nothing better; I told you to open it, just now, and you would not.... Now, now, do not weep any more.... Be reasonable. ... I am old too, but I am reasonable. Now, now, do not weep any more....

QUEEN.
There, there; it is over; I will weep no more, I will weep no more.... They must not hear me weeping when they wake...
.
KING.
Come, come, I shall open the door very softly; we will go in together.... *He tries to open the door; the lock grates, and, inside the hall, the latch can be seen to lift and fall back again.* Oh, oh! what is the matter with the lock, I wonder?—I cannot open the door... push a little.... 1 do not know what it can be.... I did not know it was so hard to get into this hall. ... Will you try? *Tlie* Queen *tries in her turn, without success.* It does not open.... I believe they have drawn the bolts.... Yes, yes; the door is locked; it will not open....
QUEEN.
They always lock it.... Oh, oh! do not abandon them so!... They have slept so long!
PRINCE.
We might open a window....
KING.
The windows do not open.
PRINCE.
It seems to me it is not so light in the hall....
KING.
It is just as light there; but the sky is clearing. — Do you see the stars?
PRINCE.
What shall we do?
KING.
I do not know.... —There is another entrance... PRINCE.
There is another entrance?
QUEEN.
No! no! I know what you mean!... Not that way! not that way! I will not go down!...
KING.
We will not go down; we will stay here; Marcellus will go alone....
QUEEN.
Oh, no, no, no!... Let us wait....
KING.
But, after all, what will you have us do? — There is no other way to get into the hall... that is as clear as possible....
PRINCE.
There is another entrance?

KING.

Yes; there is still a little entrance... you cannot see it from here... but you will easily find it. You must go down underneath-.. PRINCE.

Where must I go down?

KING.

Come here. *He draivs him a little aside.* It is not a door... you could not call it a door... it is a trap, rather... it is a movable slab in the floor. It is quite at the back of the hall.... You must go through the vaults... you understand.... Then come up again.... You' will need a lamp... you might lose yourself... you might dash yourself against the... the marble... do you understand?... Take care; there are chains between the... the little passages.... But you should know the way.... You went down there more than once formerly....

PRINCE.

I went down there more than once formerly?

KING.

Why, yes; why, yes; where your mother...

PRINCE.

Where my mother...?— Ah, is it there I must go?...

KING. *Makes a sign with his head.* 'Tit is there. — And where your father also...

PRINCE.

Yes, yes; I remember... and where others also...

KING.

You understand!... The stone is not cemented; you have only to push a little... . But be careful.... There are some slabs that are not regular.... Be on your guard for a bust that bends its head a little across the path... it is marble.... There is a cross, too, with arms a little long... be on your guard... do not hurry; you have plenty of time....

PRINCE.

And it is there I must go?...

KING.

It is there!... He must have a lamp. *He goes to the edge of the terrace and calls.* A lamp! a lamp! a little lamp ... *To the* Prince. We will wait here at the windows.... We are too old to go down there.... We could not climb up again. ... _*A lighted lamp is brought.* Ah, ah, here

is the lamp; take the little lamp....

PRINCE.

Yes, yes; the little lamp....

At this moment great cries of joy from the sailors are heard suddenly without. The masts, yards, and sails of the ship are illuminated, in the midst of the darkness, on the horizon of the canal, among the willows KING.

Oh, oh, what is that?

PRINCE.

It is the sailors.... They are dancing on the bridge; they are tipsy....

KING.

They have lighted up the ship....

PRINCE.

It is the joy of departure.... They are just leaving....

KING.

Well, will you go down?... It is this way.

QUEEN.

No, no, do not go there!... Do not go that way!... do not wake them! do not wake them!... You know they must have rest!. .. I am afraid!...

PRINCE.

I will not wake the others, if you wish... . I will wake one only....

QUEEN.

Oh 1 oh! oh!

KING.

Make no noise as you enter....

PRINCE.

I am afraid they will not recognize me.. ..

KING.

There is no danger.... Eh, eh! take care of the little lamp!... Don't you see there is a wind?... the wind will blow it out!...

PRINCE.

I fear they will not all wake at once.

KING.

What does that matter?... Do not wake them roughly, that is all.

PRINCE.

I shall be all alone before them.... I shall look as if... they will be afraid....

KING.

You will only wake them after putting the stone back in its place.... They will not notice anything.... They do not know what there is under the hall where they sleep....

PRINCE.

They will take me for a stranger....

KING.

We will be at the windows. — Go down; go down. — Take care of the lamp. — Above all, do not lose yourself in the vaults; they are of a great depth.... Be careful to put the slab back.... Come up as soon as possible.... We will wait at the windows.... Go down, go down; — careful! careful!...

The Prince leaves the terrace; the old King and the old Queen look through the windows, with their faces against the panes. — A long silence.

FAR-AWAY VOICES.

The Atlantic! The Atlantic!

KING. *Turning his head and looking toward the canal.* Ah, ah! they are going.. .. They will have a fair wind to-night....

FAR-AWAY VOICES.

We shall return no more! We shall return no more!

KING. *Looking toward the canal.* They will be on the open sea before midnight. ... VOICES. *Farther and farther away.* The Atlantic! The Atlantic! KING. *Looking into the hall.* If only he does not lose himself in the darkness.... VOICES. *Almost inaudible.* We shall return no more! We shall return no more!

A silence; the ship disappears among the willows KING.

Looking toward the canal. You cannot see them any longer. — *Looking into the hall.* He has not come yet? — *Looking toward the canal.* — The ship is no longer there! — *To the* Queen. — You pay no attention? — You do not answer? — Where are you? Look at the canal. — They have gone; they will be on the open sea before midnight.... QUEEN. *Distractedly* They will be on the open sea before midnight.... KING. *Looking into the hall.* Can you see the slab he should lift? — It is covered with inscriptions; — it must be hidden by the laurels. — He has grown tall, Marcellus, has he not? — We would have done better to wake them before he landed — I told you so. — We should have avoided all these scenes. — I do not know why he did not look happy this evening. — They were wrong to draw the bolts; I will have them taken off. — If only his lamp does not go out! — Where are you? — Do you see anything? — Why do you not answer? — If only he does not lose himself in the darkness! — Are you listening to me? QUEEN.

If only he does not lose himself in the darkness!...

KING.

You are right. — Do you not find it is beginning to grow cold? — They will be cold on the marble. — It seems to me he is taking his time. — If only his little lamp does not go out! — Why do you not answer? What are you dreaming about?

QUEEN.

If only his little lamp...! The stone! the stone! the stone!...

KING.

Is he there? —Is he coming in? —I cannot see that far....

QUEEN.

It rises! it rises!... There is a light!... look... listen! listen! — It creaks on its hinges!...

KING.

I told him to go in very softly....

QUEEN.

Oh, he is coming in very softly.... See, see, he is putting his hand through with the lamp....

KING.

Yes, yes; I see the little lamp.... Why does he not enter at once?...

QUEEN.

He cannot.... He is lifting the stone very slowly.... Yes, yes; very slowly... Oh, how it creaks! how it creaks! how it creaks!... They will wake with a start!

KING.

I cannot see very well what is going on. .. I know the stone is very heavy....

QUEEN.

He enters... He comes up... He comes up more and more slowly... Oh, but the stone cries now!... oh, oh! it cries! it cries! It wails like a child!... He is half in the hall!... Three steps more! three steps more! *Clapping her hands,.* He is in the hall! He is in the hall!... Look! look!... They wake!... They all wake with a start!...

KING.

Has he let the slab fall?

The Prince, letting go the sepulchral slab he has just lifted, stops, lamp in hand, at the foot of the marble steps. Six

of the princesses, at the last gratin? of the hinges, open their eyes, stir a moment on the edge of sleep, and then rise simultaneously at his approach, their arms raised in slow attitudes of waking. One only. Ursula, remains stretched on her back on the marble steps, motionless, in the midst of her sisters, who exchange with the Prince a long look full of marvellings, bewilderments and silences.) QUEEN.

At the windows. Ursula! Ursula! Ursula!... She does not wake!... KING.

Patience! patience! — She sleeps a little heavily....

QUEEN. *Crying out, her face against the windows!* Ursula! Ursula! — Wake her! *Knocking on the windows.* Marcellus! Marcellus! — Wake her! Wake her too! Ursula! Ursula!... Marcellus! Marcellus!... She has not heard!... Ursula! Ursula! Arise! He is there! He is there!... It is time! It is time! — *Knocking at another window* Marcellus! Marcellus! Look before you! look! She is sleeping still!... *Knocking at another window!* — Oh, oh! — Christabel! Christabel! Claribel! Claribel!... Clara! Clara! Oh, Clara!... She has not heard!... *Knocking constantly and violently on the windows* Ursula! Ursula! He has come back! He is there! He is there!... It is time! It is time!... KING. _Also knocking at the windows._ Yes; yes; wake her!... Oh, wake her!... We are waiting....

The Prince, unheeding the noises outside, approaches in silence the one who has not risen. He gazes upon her a moment, hesitates, bends his knee and touches one of the arms lying bare and inert on the silken cushions. At the contact of the flesh he rises suddenly, with a long and sweeping look of terror at the six princesses, who remain mute and are extremely pale. They, at first undecided and trembling with the desire to flee, stoop finally with a unanimous movement over their prostrate sister, lift her, and, in the deepest silence, bear the body, already rigid, with head dishevelled and stiff, to the highest of the seven marble steps; while the Queen, the King, and the people of the chateau, who have hurried to the scene, knock and cry out violently at all the windows

of the hall: these two scenes take place simultaneously.

QUEEN.

She is not asleep! She is not asleep! — It is not sleep! It is not sleep! It is no longer sleep! *She runs desperately from window to window; she knocks at them, she shakes the iron bars; she stamps and her white unknotted hair is seen quivering against the panes.* She is no longer sleeping, I tell you! 7i *the* King. Oh! oh! oh! you are a man of stone!... Cry out! cry out! cry out! For God's sake! cry out, I tell you! I scream myself to death and he does not understand! — Run! run! cry! cry! He has seen nothing! nothing! nothing! nothing! never! never! never!...

KING. . What? what? What is it? What is it? Where must I cry out? QUEEN.

Down there! down there! Everywhere! everywhere! on the terrace! over the water! over the meadows!... Cry! cry! cry!...

On the edge of the terrace. Oh!... oh!... Hurry! hurry! here! here!... Ursula! Ursula!... There is something the matter!... QUEEN. *At the windows.* Ursula! Ursula!... Pour some water on her!... — Yes, yes, do that, my child... It is perhaps not...!Oh, oh, oh!... her little head!... *Servitors, soldiers, peasants, women, run up on the terrace with torches and lanterns* Ursula! Ursula!.... It is perhaps not that... It may be nothing at all!... Eh! eh! Claribel! Claribel! Take care!... She will fall!... Do not tread on her hair!... Open! open! — She will wake! she will wake!... water! water! water! — Open! open! the door! the door 1 the door!... No one can get in! Everything is locked! everything is locked!... You are deaf as dead folk ... *To those about her.* Help me! — You are horrible people! My hands!... My hands!... You see my hands?... Help me! help me! Oh, oh! It is late!... It is too late?... It is too late!... closed! closed! closed!... ALL. *Shaking the door and knocking at all the windows.* Open! open! open! open!...

A black curtain falls brusquely.

PRINTED BY R. R. DONNELLEY AND SONS COMPANY, AT THE LAKESIDE PRESS, CHICAGO, ILL. i in if iiiliiiii if ill "" 3 9015 OI339ISIP

CPSIA information can be obtained at www.ICGtesting.com
Printed in the USA
BVOW09s1032140714

359105BV00021B/899/P